JAMES W. McLAMORE

January 14, 1988

Dear Bill:

I understand a group of good friends will be helping Murry Evans celebrate his 50th birthday. I wish I could be there because Murry has always been one of my favorite people.

It doesn't seem possible this "young kid" is 50. In fact, I remember the first time I met him. He wasn't even 25! But he was impressive. He gave me the feeling from the very beginning that he was determined to do something important with his life. This was no ordinary "kid". This was a young man with a purpose. You could tell he would succeed in anything he set his mind to. Perhaps that is the reason we gambled a bit on the guy. He certainly didn't have any financial means to speak of, but when it came to other collateral, he had plenty of that. Plenty of class, a lot of determination and a style you simply had to like.

I'm glad he came Burger King's way. He lived up to his promise. Murry is a true leader. He has proven that. He is a credit to his family, his friends, community and employees. What I fully expected of him he has delivered. He has created a major business success story while, at the same time, remaining humble and appreciative of the help he received along the way. The short of it all is that he is simply a neat guy.

So, on the day of his 50th celebration, tell him hello from his friend and admirer, Jim, and wish him well. I'll be with all of you in spirit wishing I was there.

Sincerely,

Jim McLamore

Mr. William R. Spence, Jr.
4401 Gulfshore Boulevard, North
Apartment 501
Naples, Florida 33940

SOUTHEAST BANK BUILDING, SUITE 211, 7100 NORTH KENDALL DRIVE, MIAMI, FLORIDA 33156
TELEPHONE: (305) 667-1044

Letter from Jim McLamore, co-founder of Burger King, to his son-in-law, Bill Spence, to be read at Murry's 50th birthday celebration. Bill was a Burger King franchisee with 35 restaurants at the time and a close friend of Murry's.

POVERTY TO RICHES
—*My Way!*

HOW I MADE MILLIONS

Murry J. Evans

Copyright © 2013 by Numedia LTD

All rights reserved. No portion of this book may be copied or reproduced in any form, except for short passages quoted in reviews, without prior written permission from the author.

Book Editing & Design:
Cara Stein / BookCompletion.com

Why You Need to Read this Book

Why should you read this book? It's simple: because I've done what you want to do. I started with no money, and I went from losing $20,000 in my first year of business to owning 69 Burger King stores, drawing a $1 million salary, flying in a private Lear Jet, and making a $2.4 million bottom-line profit.

I'm a real person; I'm not any different than you. I'm not a phony or a con man. I'm a poor boy who started with nothing, just a desire to succeed and to have something.

I was poor, and I felt like there had to be something better than being poor. I wanted to be rich. Well, you don't get rich overnight—you have to work at it.

I built my business a day at a time with my bare hands. I'm not a Hollywood actor, and I didn't play building an empire of 69 Burger Kings. I wasn't acting; it was the real thing.

From college students to professors who teach business

and entrepreneurship, I've had hundreds of people ask me personally, "How did you do it, Murry? How did you become successful?"

They want to know the story. This book is my answer.

In this book, I will cover 36 years of my business life, from the first Burger King to the 69th: how I chose restaurant sites, built a team, marketed my stores, and added breakfast service to my stores.

I almost went bankrupt three times—absolutely bankrupt. How did I come out of it? I'll cover that in the book.

The story begins when I was a boy. I was born into a poor family. My father died when I was 13 years old, and I went to work to try to support my mom and my two sisters, still having to go to school.

Just like you, I knew I wanted to be successful. I wanted to own my own business, but I realized I was on my own. Regardless of the conditions I found myself in, I was responsible for building my own success. By the grace of God, I was able to do that.

It wasn't easy. It took work and dedication. It took a team.

I succeeded, and you can, too. If you're in business and trying to make it work, I can relate. I understand starting a business, growing the business, and finally, selling the business for millions. I've been there and done that.

It doesn't just happen. You have to make it happen. I'll cover how I did it in this book—what worked for me personally. I hope it will motivate you to be successful.

Now, you can't put me in a round hole or a square hole. I'm sure that if you're reading this, people try to put you in a round or square hole, don't they? They always do. People will ask you questions to decide where to put you, and once they can get you in a hole, they've got you! They think they know everything about you and how you operate.

Well, people don't know how I operate. I march to a different drummer. I'm sure you do, also.

I'm not another "how to make millions" story. I'm not a "me, too" individual. I fit no mold.

My stories are true stories. I'm a real person, and I really did this, one day at a time. I built a multi-million dollar business that afforded me an unbelievable lifestyle. As other people saw my success, they came and visited me in Mobile, Alabama, wanting my advice. They wanted help in being successful.

The number-one question people ask me is how I did it, and I'm going to tell it to you just like it happened. I pray that you can use some of the points that I used, and that some of

A quick photo moment before returning home to Mobile, Alabama, from a business meeting in Florida. From left: Murry, his wife Marilyn, son Mark, chief pilot Bill Gray, and co-pilot.

the things that worked for me will work for you.

Very few people have a story worth reading, worth telling, or worth listening to. I am the exception. This will be worth your time and money.

This should motivate you. I graduated in the bottom third of my high school class. If a guy like me can be successful, anyone has a chance at success. So here's my story: how I did it—*my way!*

Contents

Why You Need to Read this Book iii

The First Basic Principle of Business: Time and Money 1

The #1 Key to Success: Find What you Love to Do 5

Learn from Steve Jobs: Connecting the Dots, or Time
and Chance 15

The Start of a Restaurant Empire: How I found Burger King ... 25

Success Secret #2: Use Your Brains and Someone Else's
Hands and Money 31

Location, Location, Location: Choosing the Right City 41

Success Secret #3: Cause Something to Happen 45

The Foundation of any Successful Business: Building a Great
Team 61

When the Experts are Wrong: Buying a Pig in a Poke and
Making Millions 85

The Genius of Execution: Getting the Most out of People
Smarter than You 109

The Danger of Playing it Safe: Burger King's Double
Drive-Thru 117

Five-Cent Jelly: How Hardee's Unwittingly Helped Me
Add Breakfast 123

Brand or Traffic Marketing: Two of My Most Successful
Promotions, and Corporate's Surprising Response 127

How to Make Money: Add Value and Control Cost 135

Poverty to Riches: Selling for Millions 149

About the Author 155

CHAPTER 1

The First Basic Principle of Business:

Time and Money

One of the first lessons I learned as a Burger King franchisee was the principle of **time and money**. I learned it from Jim McLamore, one of the co-founders of Burger King Corporation.

After I put down the deposit for my first franchise, Jim McLamore said, "Murry, I want to tell you something. Always remember that people have two things to spend: time and money."

He looked at me and asked me, "Which one do you think they'd rather spend?"

Of course, being a poor boy, I thought, "Well... time, because man... you don't have much money."

I was wrong. I was 100% wrong.

People would rather spend their money than their time. If you think about it, it's true. Here's why: You can work and get more money, but you can never get more time.

This principle is important in any business—I don't care what it is. If you order something online, you want it tomorrow, don't you? Actually, you'd like it today!

We applied the time and money principle at all of my Burger King stores. At the time, Burger King advertised 60-second service. In other words, you came to the window, you ordered your Whopper, fries, Coke, milkshake… and within 60 seconds, you'd have it in your hands.

Well, I went a little bit further with that. I was taught by one of their managers, Ed Healy, a retired Master Sergeant in the Army. He had tremendously fast reflexes, and he taught me all of the tricks of the trade on how to assemble the orders quickly and get the food to the customer in the shortest time possible. None of what he taught me was written in the Burger King operations manual. It was expert knowledge, received directly from Ed Healy himself.

General Manager Hardie Cazalas quickly assembling a customer's order to be served in an average of 12 seconds.

POVERTY TO RICHES—MY WAY

We would use a stopwatch to time our service times at lunch, because people had a minimum amount of time at lunch. People don't mind spending their money if they're getting value and convenience. The primary consideration is not how much it costs, it's "how fast can you give it to me?"

Instead of the 60 seconds Burger King was advertising, we would average 12 seconds per person. Now that's fast! But we did it.

We had a system set up. We worked at it, and we had a reputation in Mobile, Alabama, as well as the other cities where we had stores. Fast service is the number-one thing we pushed. People want to pay their money, get their food, and go.

I'll tell you a story about that. In Gulf Shores, Alabama, I opened a Burger King, and it just did tremendously. I got the prime spot there. McDonald's came along later; they had missed it, so they had to go down on the beach and take a secondary location.

One day, I walked into my Gulf Shores store. My manager said, "Mr. Evans, I want to tell you a story. Just last week, one of our customers came in and said that he'd stopped by the McDonald's down at the beach for a quick bite. He was sitting there eating his burger, and he heard two people talking.

"He realized they were McDonald's supervisors. They were talking about the service and how bad it was there. One of them got up and said to the other one, 'Let's go down to the Burger King, where we can get some fast service!'"

Even the McDonald's supervisors knew that Burger King had a reputation for giving fast service.

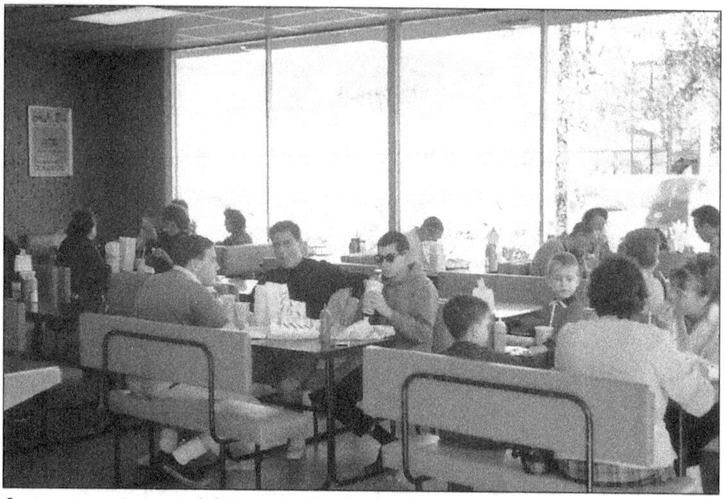

Customers enjoying a delicious meal at Burger King.

CHAPTER 2

The #1 Key to Success: Find What You Love To Do

What do you love to do? What type of work do you enjoy doing and have a passion for? It's an important question to ask yourself. Many people don't know the answer, but it's the key to being successful—and happy. I was speaking to a group of business students working on their master's degrees in Kuala Lumpur, Malaysia, about six months ago, and I asked them this question.

Some kids just didn't know. Some had blank looks. But one young man spoke up and said, "I love interior design."

I asked what he was doing now. It wasn't interior design; he was doing whatever he could to put bread on the table.

When I told him he ought to do interior design, his face lit up. He had been doing it on his own, but he never thought he could make a living at it.

I said, "Now, don't quit your day job, but go get a job working with an interior design company, and read all you can about interior design. If that's your passion, you will make a living at it."

Steve Jobs talked about the same thing in his commencement address to Stanford University graduates on June 12, 2005. Steve Jobs was the CEO of Apple Computer and Pixar Animation Studios. In his speech, he said, "I was lucky. I found what I loved to do early in life. Woz and I started Apple in my parents' garage when I was 20."

He went on to talk about building Apple and then being fired from his own company. He said he thought his world had caved in, but he realized, "I still loved what I did. The turn of events at Apple had not changed that one bit. I had been rejected, but I was still in love, so I decided to start over."

Here's a man who realized he still loved what he was doing (working with computers), so he went out and started NeXT Computer and Pixar, which produced the first computer-animated movie: *Toy Story*. He said, "Don't lose faith. I'm convinced that the only thing that kept me going was that I loved what I did."

You know, he's right on. This is exactly what I tell people all the time: find out what it is that you love doing and have a passion for, and do it! Don't let anyone get in your way—do it!

It worked for Steve Jobs. He loved what he did. He had adversity come along—he got fired! Was he going to change? He considered getting out of the industry, but he realized this was what he loved, so he decided to stay in it.

In his speech, he said, "You've got to find what you love. That is as true for your work as it is for your lovers. Your work is going to fill a large part of your life, and the only way to be truly satisfied is to do what you believe is great work. And the only way to do great work is to love what you do.

"If you haven't found it yet, keep looking, and don't settle. As with all matters of the heart, you'll know when you find it. And, like any great relationship, it just gets better and better as the years roll on. So keep looking. Don't settle."

I agree with him 100%. Find out what it is that you love to do, and do it.

I found what I loved at a very young age, but I didn't know it would become my life's work. As I look back on my life and realize what I loved doing, I'll tell you the truth: I loved making sandwiches.

I loved taking two pieces of bread and making a sandwich, whether it was a cucumber and mayonnaise sandwich, or peanut butter and jelly, or plain peanut butter, or plain jelly. I loved making a bologna sandwich; or salami; lettuce and tomato; liverwurst; ham and cheese; or burgers. We didn't have too many burgers because beef was expensive and we were poor, but any kind of leftovers that I could make a sandwich out of, I made into a sandwich.

My dad got paid every Saturday, and by Wednesday, we were out of most of the things he had bought on Saturday at the grocery store. We were out of bologna, salami, peanut butter and jelly... By the end of the week, all we had left was bread, so we just made jam sandwiches.

Once, I told this story to someone, and they asked me, "What kind of jam did you use—grape jam? Strawberry?"

I said, "No, we just jammed two pieces of bread together and ate it! That's how poor we were." I want to tell you, it was good, too—jam sandwiches.

I found out early, I loved sandwiches. The other thing I enjoyed doing as a kid was cooking french fries. As early as eight or nine years old, I'd ask my dad after supper if I could cut up some Irish potatoes and cook some fries in the iron skillet. He'd generally say, "Yeah, go ahead."

I'd cook those fries. I'd get some ketchup, and I'd sit there and eat the entire pile of fries that I'd cooked up. I love french fries, and I love sandwiches.

Little did I know, I'd be doing that for my life's work. But I got lucky. Steve Jobs said he got lucky by getting into what he loved doing at 20 years old. I got lucky and found Burger King at 24. I had my own store by the time I was 25 years old.

When I saw Burger King, I said, "This is it! I am in love. This is what I want to do the rest of my life." And I meant it.

It was like that with my wife, too. I was in eighth grade

Murry's first Burger King, store #129, under construction at 2959 Springhill Avenue, Mobile, Alabama, September 1963.

when I first saw my future wife. I didn't even know her name. I just saw this girl standing over there, and I said to myself, "I'm going to marry her."

And you know what? I did! It was a little bit later, after I graduated from college, but I was in love. I'll tell you, as Steve Jobs says, it just gets better as the years roll by. We're still in love.

One thing I did do, I'll have to confess: I married an older woman. She's 11 days older than I.

When you find what you love, go after it. That's what I did with my wife, and that's what I did with Burger King.

Once, a group of franchisees that I belonged to invited a man to come and present a personality profile test. The test had a series of questions, and for each question, you would mark a number from one to five, with five meaning this point was very true for you. In one column, you'd answer these questions for your current job, and in the other column, you'd answer them for your ideal job. Then you'd add up the two columns, and the closer the totals were, the closer you were to being in your ideal job.

It took about 30 minutes. I added all the numbers up on the left, and I think I got 73. I added up all the numbers on the right: 73 in that column, too.

I didn't quite understand what that meant, so I raised my hand and asked the fellow. He said, "That's fantastic! That means you are doing exactly what you enjoy doing."

I said, "Man, I could've told you that before I took the test! You just wasted 30 minutes of my time. If you wanted to know that, I could've told you that." Of course, everyone laughed.

I've been asked, "How could you open a second store while

the first one was going broke?" Well, most people wouldn't. But I was passionate about what I was doing.

I knew the concept was a success, and I was doing okay until McDonald's opened up about three months after I did. For the first three months, I was doing well. I was on the way to making money the first year. For most businesses, you can't expect to make money that quickly, but it wasn't unusual in the early days of fast food. Many times, you'd put up a fast food restaurant, and it just did tremendously.

My first Burger King store started out like that, but when the McDonald's opened nearby, we started losing money. If I didn't truly love what I was doing, I would have gone bankrupt. I would have thrown in the towel; I wouldn't have had a second store. And you wouldn't be reading this book, because I wouldn't be writing it.

It took a few years before I started making money at the first store. I got it to break even around the third year, but I didn't really make money at that store for about five years. But because I loved what I was doing, I stuck with it. I opened the second store, and I started making money there.

Many people ask me for advice on situations like this. A few months ago, I was speaking to nearly 300 university students in a lecture room. It was standing room only. I spoke for about 30 minutes, and then I opened it up for questions.

A young lady asked, "How do you keep going when adversity strikes?"

That was about the third time one of the students had asked that question, and I had already answered it, but they were afraid of adversity. I could tell they were terrified of failure and the problems that come up in business. The group

POVERTY TO RICHES—MY WAY

wanted to know how to handle it.

My answer is very simple: you have to love what you're doing. If you love what you're doing, you will increase your chance of survival and maximize your income. And, as a side benefit, you'll never work a day in your life. In 36 years, I never worked a day, I guarantee.

Don't do something to get rich. Don't open a business as an electrician or an engineer or a doctor because you think that's where the money is. You'll be miserable and probably fail. Even if you succeed, you will not enjoy life.

Life is more than money. Life is short—ask Steve Jobs!

Take his advice. Enjoy what you do, and you will enjoy your life. I'm telling you the same thing. Please listen to us. Do what you love.

I had the opportunity to tell this to one young lady back in 1993. It was October 16, the 30th anniversary of starting my first Burger King. I said to my wife, "Marilyn, we've been

The sign at Murry's first Burger King, store #129, which opened on October 16, 1963.

in business 30 years. Let's go have a Whopper and celebrate!"

She laughed and said, "All right, let's go."

So we went over to the original store. I had rebuilt the original store about three blocks down the street. I bought a shopping center and sold most of it, but I kept the prime corner location and built a new Burger King. So we went there to celebrate our 30th anniversary.

Before I ordered my sandwiches, I went into the back room. I'd always go back there and speak to the team members, shake the manager's hand, see how everything was going, and let them know I appreciated the job they were doing.

While I was back there, I passed a young lady who was taking orders for the drive-thru. I read her name tag, and I said, "Hey, Sally, how are you doing? Are you having fun?"

She said, "Not really."

I said, "If you're not having fun, you need to go do something else."

She had an order coming in, so she turned and took the order. I went out and ordered our Whoppers.

We enjoyed a delicious meal: Whopper, fries, and a Coke. But Sally in the drive-thru stayed on my mind. If she wasn't having any fun, I wanted to get her off the drive-thru, because I didn't want her irritating any of our customers.

After we finished eating, I went back in, but I didn't see her. I asked the manager, "Hey, where's Sally, the young lady who was working the drive-thru?"

He said, "She quit. She told me you told her that if she wasn't having fun, she ought to go do something else, that life was short."

I was surprised, but that was exactly what I had told her.

POVERTY TO RICHES—MY WAY

He said, "She told me, 'I'm not having fun, so I quit.'"

I said, "That's good! Now she's happy—she's going to go find something she enjoys doing. That's what she should do. And we're also ahead of the game because she's not making our customers unhappy with an unhappy attitude."

Absolutely, do what you love. Be like the girl at store #129—if you're not happy and having fun, go find what you love.

CHAPTER 3

Learn from Steve Jobs:

Connecting the Dots, or Time and Chance

Doing what you love is important, and so is another point from Steve Jobs's commencement address: connecting the dots. He said that as he got older and looked back on his life, he realized things had come together and connected in a way that he couldn't have predicted when he was young.

For example, Steve Jobs dropped out of Reed College after six months because he felt he was wasting his parents' money. He didn't want them to spend their life savings on his college tuition, when he didn't really see where his education was going.

Once he dropped out, he stopped taking required courses and started sitting in on classes that interested him. As it happened, Reed College had one of the best calligraphy courses in the country, and Steve Jobs dropped in and learned all about letterforms and typography. He just did it because he found it interesting, but later, he used what he learned in that class to design typography into the Macintosh.

If he hadn't dropped out of college, he never would have known about typography. The Mac wouldn't have had the fonts it did, and other personal computers might never have gotten them, either. He realized that somehow those dots were connected in his past. You can look back and see it in the past, but you can't see it being done in the future.

Looking back, he realized that a lot of things that seemed bad at the time actually turned out to be a blessing to him. When he got fired from Apple, it felt terrible at the time, but when he looked back, he said it was the greatest thing that happened to him. He went out and started a new company called NeXT, and then he started Pixar. He had a tremendous time with development and creating things—doing what he loved doing.

So, he connected the dots in his life and saw how things had worked out in the past. In his commencement address, he said, "Of course, it was impossible to connect the dots looking forward when I was in college. But it was very, very clear, looking backwards 10 years later."

He's right: you can't connect the dots looking forward. You can only connect them looking backwards. When he finally realized that the dots were connected in his past, he realized the dots would also be connected in his future.

He didn't know who was connecting those dots. Well, I know who's connecting the dots for me: the Lord is, and He's using time and chance.

"Time and chance" comes from Ecclesiastes. It was written by King Solomon, the wisest man who ever lived.

POVERTY TO RICHES—MY WAY

"I returned, and saw under the sun, that the race is not to the swift, nor the battle to the strong, neither yet bread to the wise, nor yet riches to men of understanding, nor yet favor to men of skill; but time and chance happeneth to them all." —Ecclesiastes 9:11

Steve Jobs calls it connecting the dots; the Bible calls it time and chance. It happens to everybody. As things happen in your life, some feel good, and some feel bad. But they all work out for good in the end, even though it might not seem like it at the time.

Steve Jobs said, "During those times, you have to trust that the dots will somehow connect in your future. You have to trust in something: your gut, destiny, life, karma, whatever you can trust in. This approach has never let me down, and it has made all the difference in my life."

Now, I trust in the Lord that things will work out in my life, and they certainly have. Looking back, it's easy to connect the dots and see how time and chance were working in my life, though I couldn't see it at the time. Here's how it happened in my life to bring me to Burger King.

My senior year in high school, I was delivering the *St. Petersburg Times* morning newspaper. I woke up around 2:30 a.m. each morning to go to the newspaper office in Bradenton, Florida. I rolled my papers and delivered them on my motorbike.

One Sunday morning, I had a headache. When the alarm sounded at 2:30, I got up, took two aspirin, and lay back down to give the headache a chance to recede.

I didn't intend to go to sleep, but I did. The phone rang around 3:30—the manager wanted to know where I was. I said, "I'll be right there, I'll be right there!"

I asked my mom if I could drive the car down. On Sunday mornings, we had big papers, so I'd have to take four or five trips on the motorbike to get all of the papers delivered. If I could use the car, then I put all of them in the back seat and delivered them in one trip. That was a lot faster, and I was already late.

It was only about one time in 10 that my mom would let me use the car on Sunday morning. This Sunday morning, she did. Remember, time and chance.

So, I got in the car and drove down to the office. I went to the back and started rolling papers, getting ready to deliver them. In this office, I was the only kid who delivered papers. All the carriers were adults except me.

As I rolled my papers, there was a man waiting in the front part of the office. When the manager walked in, he shook the man's hand and said, "Oh, Mr. Chapman, how are you, sir?"

Then the manager introduced me. He said, "This is Mr. Chapman, the vice president of the *St. Petersburg Times.*" I realized he was important. Mr. Alva H. Chapman, Jr., ran the day-to-day operations of the *St. Petersburg Times.* He was general manager and vice president.

He asked if he could ride with me while I delivered my papers.

I said, "Yes sir, no problem."

As I delivered the papers, Mr. Chapman asked me questions about myself. He asked if I planned to attend college.

I said, "I don't have any money."

He said, "What college would you attend if you had the money?"

I said, "The Citadel, the Military College of South Carolina, located in Charleston."

He about fell out of the car. He graduated from The Citadel!

Very few young men wanted to go to a military college—they'd rather go to a university with fun and games. He asked why I wanted to go there.

I said, "Well, I'm just an ordinary poor guy. I wear ordinary clothes. I can see that everybody at The Citadel wears the same uniform, so I'm sure they judge you, not by the clothes you wear, but on performance." That was 100% correct—they do.

Mr. Chapman helped me get a Kiwanis Club gift scholarship, and he also wrote to the Pickett and Hatcher Loan Foundation in Columbus, Georgia, to set up an arrangement for me to borrow $700 for my first year.

My first year of college cost me a little over $1300, and the Kiwanis Club scholarship was $500 per year for four years. My total cost to go to college, including tuition, room and board, clothes, and everything was about $4,500 for four years.

Mr. Chapman, the vice president of the *St. Petersburg Times*, helped me get the Kiwanis Club scholarship by vouching for me to Mr. C. C. Carter, the chairman of the scholarship committee.

I applied for the scholarship, along with other students. It was awarded based on your school record and on need.

I had a strong school record. Although my grades weren't the best, I was vice president of the senior class, president of the M Club, and a member of the Western Conference championship football team. I was also on the basketball team and the track team, and I participated in the Key Club, the student council, and the senior play. And I certainly had the need.

Later, Mr. Carter told me that he called Mr. Chapman about it. He said, "Look, we want to give the scholarship to Murry Evans, but he's so poor—his family has no money—we're afraid it won't be used."

Mr. Chapman said, "You go ahead and give it to him. Betty and I will guarantee he gets the rest of the money." (Betty was his wife.)

I confronted Mr. Chapman with that about 35 years later, when my wife and I were having dinner with him and his wife in Miami, Florida. He smiled and said, "That's correct."

It's time and chance. You don't know what's happening or why at the time. It's the Lord, working things out, connecting the dots for you... Time and chance.

So, how did I get to Miami? Well, Mr. Chapman had

General Mark Wayne Clark presenting Murry his diploma on graduation day, June 4, 1960.

POVERTY TO RICHES—MY WAY

Murry and Marilyn on the parade ground at The Citadel after graduation. They were married six days later, on June 10, 1960.

bought the *Savannah Morning News* and the *Evening Press* in Savannah, Georgia. He had it for three years, and then, my senior year in college, he had to sell it. He had offered me a job in Savannah, but after he sold the paper there, he moved to Miami and offered me a job at the *Miami Herald*. That's how I moved to Miami, not Savannah.

About six months after I got to Miami, I ran into Burger King.

The dots had connected, starting with my headache that Sunday morning. Since I was late going down to the newspaper office, all the adults had already rolled their papers and gone. The manager told me later that if there had been one adult there, he would not have had Mr. Chapman ride with me—he would have certainly put him with a mature adult.

Not only that, my mom let me use the car that Sunday. If she hadn't, well, Mr. Chapman and I certainly could not have ridden on my motorbike.

The other thing is that Mr. Chapman overslept! He was

supposed to be there an hour earlier. Since he was late, he decided not to go, but his wife said, "No, go," so he listened to his wife.

You know, there are times when you're supposed to listen to your wife. He was late, and if he'd been on time, he would have gone with one of the adults. I never would have talked to him, and I wouldn't have had that connection to go to Miami to find Burger King.

Also, it turned out that he had graduated from the college I wanted to go to. He also graduated from the same high school in Bradenton, Florida.

He guaranteed the extra money that I would need, assuring C. C. Carter that I would use the entire Kiwanis Club scholarship if it were awarded to me. He found the Pickett and Hatcher Loan Foundation out of Columbus, Georgia, that lent to college students. He set up that loan for me, and he signed the loan to guarantee that I would pay it back.

The loan required three guarantors. My future father-in-law, Roy Harris, and a local businessman, Bill Manning, also signed for me. It took me about three years, but I paid it back after I graduated.

Time and chance... Connecting the dots... In Miami... In Burger King.

I had gone to work for Mr. Chapman in Miami, thinking I was going to have a career in the newspaper industry. I loved the newspaper industry, but when I ran into Burger King, I said, "This is it for me. This is what I want to do the rest of my life."

Time and chance, connecting the dots—call it what you want. It's real. It's working, and if you look backward in your life, you can see it. I highly recommend that you do, whatever age you are.

Also realize that, as Steve Jobs says, it's going to work out in the future. Just keep doing the job and keep making something happen, and those dots will be connected. Time and chance will take place, and you'll be better for it.

CHAPTER 4

The Start of a Restaurant Empire:

How I found Burger King

When I graduated from college, I went to Miami, Florida, to work in the newspaper industry. As I mentioned in the last chapter, Mr. Chapman offered me a job. I was originally going to be in Savannah, Georgia, but when he sold his newspapers there and moved to Miami, I wound up in Miami, too.

When I got to Miami, I was working for the *Miami Herald* in their management-training program. I earned $90 a week, working six days a week. Meanwhile, my wife, Marilyn, was teaching school.

I enjoyed the newspaper business. I didn't have my own business, but I still enjoyed the work, and I loved the smell of newsprint. It's a fascinating business to me.

One weekend, I got someone to cover for me on a Saturday and Sunday. My wife and I drove up to Bradenton, Florida, which was about a four-hour drive from Miami. Her mom and dad lived in Bradenton, and I had a good friend there: Dewey Eason.

People say that if you have five friends in your life, you're a rich man. I agree, and Mr. Dewey Eason is one of my five great friends. I've known Dewey since we were 14 years old. We met when I was delivering the *Tampa Tribune* in an area where he was delivering the *Bradenton Herald*. We got to know each other and became lifelong friends.

On this particular weekend, Dewey and I went fishing. We were standing on the edge of a bridge, looking down into the water, and we began to talk. He told me that his neighbor owned a Burger Queen in Bradenton and had invited him to go and help cook french fries.

Well, that caught my attention! I loved making sandwiches, and I loved cooking french fries.

Dewey told me a little bit more about Burger Queen. The main office was in Lakeland, Florida, and they patterned the

Murry and Dewey Eason. Murry and Dewey have been lifelong friends since age 14.

business after McDonald's: they had a 15-cent hamburger, a cheeseburger, french fries, shakes, and Cokes.

Dewey said, "You know, that guy showed me his profit and loss statement, and he made $27,000 last year."

I said, "$27,000!"

I was making $90 a week, which is about $4,500 a year. I said to myself, boy that would be great to own something like that. Not only that, it was sandwiches and french fries—something I loved.

I told him I'd write to Burger Queen, Henry's, and several other similar companies. I also said I'd go to Burger King in Miami and get their information. Then we'd go in on it, 50/50. He agreed.

Of course, I didn't have any money, and neither did he. We both agreed to check with our fathers-in-law and see if they had any money they'd lend us.

When I got back to Miami, I went to the Burger King office and got the information. At that time, Burger King only had about 40 stores worldwide, and 31 of them were in Miami. It was not a big company. They had a small office, and I went in and got the material. There really wasn't a lot to the material—it was very plain, very basic.

Along with the material, I also got a list of franchisees in the Miami area, and their telephone numbers. I called them and set up appointments, and then I went by and visited them. I spent time with them and asked them questions.

They were very helpful. They shared their profit and loss statements with me and showed me what they were making. It was just awesome. They were very happy with the business they had, and they were doing extremely well.

At that time, there was no book written on fast food. It was all expert knowledge. You couldn't read about it, you had to talk to the person doing it to learn it. That's what I was doing: talking to the people who had invested their money and were operating Burger King franchises.

I talked to them because I wanted to find out whether they liked what they were doing. Were they having fun? Were they making money? And they were.

I went to see Jim McLamore, one of the co-founders of Burger King. I talked to him about how I wanted a Burger King franchise. He realized I didn't have any money, so he introduced me to a couple of franchisees who were doing well and might be willing to partner with me. I went and talked to them, but that didn't work out.

I didn't want to talk to my father-in-law until the last person. I didn't want to bother him, so I tried everything else first. I talked to Charlie Krebs, a franchisee, and we tried to work something out to go to New Orleans, Louisiana. That didn't work out. I talked to several wealthy businessmen in Bradenton. I presented my business plan to them, but they weren't interested. They said, "No, that's hamburger stand stuff."

You've got to keep in mind: at that time, people looked down on the hamburger business. After we became franchisees with Burger King, several friends of Marilyn's parents commented to them, "Oh, isn't it a shame that Murry and Marilyn are wasting their college educations on a hamburger stand."

I didn't let that bother me. I knew what I wanted to do.

When it didn't work out with the other franchisees and local businessmen, I went back to talk to Jim. He said, "Why

POVERTY TO RICHES—MY WAY

don't you just go to work for me, for Burger King Corporation?"

I said, "No, I want to be a Burger King franchisee."

He looked at me, and I remember this to this day. He said, "Evans, you don't have a pot to pee in or a window to throw it out of, you are so poor."

I said, "I know, Jim. You're exactly right, but I am going to be a Burger King franchisee."

I didn't have any money, but I wasn't going to give up. I knew what I wanted to do, and I was determined to do it.

I had wanted to own my own business since I was eight years old. I loved the newspaper business, the smell of newsprint, but I knew I could never own my own newspaper. So the Lord showed me Burger King.

I had a passion for making sandwiches and cooking french fries, and you need to have a passion about what you do.

The Coral Way Burger King in Miami, a few blocks from Coral Gables, in 1963. Burger King's corporate office was on the right side of this store. Murry met here with Mr. Jim McLamore, President of Burger King Corporation, on many occasions.

Burger King filled that passion for me. As a result, as I've mentioned before, I didn't work a day in my life during that 36 years. It was a perfect fit.

Not only that, as I got older and I looked back, I realized the newspaper business was an old industry. If you're going to go into business and have a chance of maximizing your income, you do not want to get into an old industry. It'll cost you more money to get into it, you'll work night and day, and you'll make very little money on your work. You want to find a new industry, like I did.

At the time, I didn't realize that's what I was doing, but fast food was a new industry. With a new industry, it's much easier to make money. Not *easy*—it takes work and effort and sweat—but easier than an old industry.

When I found Burger King, fast food was a new industry. I found it in Miami—connecting the dots, time and chance. Remember that I went to Miami for a newspaper career, but my heart's desire was to own my own business. I didn't want to work for The Man. I wanted to work for myself.

You probably have the same desire: you want to work for yourself. Well, keep your eyes open. You don't know what the future may hold for you. You don't know where you might find that opportunity, so you've got to be on the lookout.

Don't settle for just any job, doing something just to make money. Figure out what you love doing, and do that. If you haven't found it yet, keep looking. Do something you love.

CHAPTER 5

Success Secret #2:

Use Your Brains and Someone Else's Hands and Money

Once I found Burger King, I had my horse to ride. I knew what I wanted to do; I just didn't have any money. Luckily, I remembered a principle I had learned in college.

I learned this principle in 1958, when I was studying business administration at The Citadel, The Military College of South Carolina, which is located in Charleston.

I was taking a business law class from Major Charles Lucas. Major Lucas was an entrepreneur as well as a professor—he had businesses that he operated on the side in addition to teaching school. He was always teaching us how to run a business.

I was 19 or 20 at the time, and this was one thing that really struck me. One day in class, he told us, "**Use your brains and someone else's hands and money.**"

That's what I decided to do. A Burger King franchise was

$40,000, so I set out to get $40,000.

My friend, Dewey Eason, was going to be my partner; we were going to borrow the money and go 50/50. He didn't have any money in his family, and there certainly wasn't any money in my family, so we each agreed to try to borrow it from our fathers-in-law.

I went to Marilyn's father and mother, Mr. and Mrs. Harris, and I asked them. I presented what I wanted to do and the concept, and I gave them material to read. I also invited them to come down to Miami, Florida, and see how it worked.

They made several trips to Miami to eat the Whopper and be in the stores, talk to people, and see the operations. Mr. Harris was a frugal Ohio farmer. He had only an eighth grade education—he had to go to work when he was a kid—but he was a very intelligent man.

After about four months, he agreed to lend me the $20,000 I needed for my half of the business. Awesome!

I went back and talked to Dewey. I said, "Dewey, I got my $20,000. Have you talked to your father-in-law? Will he lend you the $20,000?"

He said, "Yeah, he would, but my wife and I talked about it, and my wife doesn't want to leave Bradenton."

I could understand that. I wanted to live in Bradenton, too, and he had a good job there. He was very successful with a company there and did extremely well.

I couldn't fault him, but now I didn't just need $20,000, I needed $40,000!

I didn't know what to do. I had to come up with a plan—it was all up to me now.

I decided to go back to my father-in-law and offer him a

deal. I said, "Okay, Dad, let's do this: let's be 50/50 partners. You put up the whole $40,000, but I'll just owe you $20,000. I'll pay you back the $20,000 with interest, and we'll be 50/50 partners."

He thought about it, and he said, "Okay."

As I worked on setting up the business, I decided I'd better buy some life insurance. That way, in case anything happened to me, Marilyn would at least have some money. I met with an insurance salesman named Harper Davidson. He was with New York Life, and I bought $100,000 worth of term life insurance from him.

As we were talking, he asked me some questions about who I was going to go into business with and what I was going to do. I told him about it. Of course, he was familiar with Burger King.

He said, "And your partner's going to be your father-in-law?"

When I said yes, he asked how old he was, and I told him 73.

He said, "He's in good health?"

I said, "Not really, and he's had a stroke."

He said, "Well, does he have any life insurance, to pay the estate taxes at his death?"

I knew his statement of worth—with him being my partner, I had to turn that in to Burger King. I said, "No, he's got $10,000 worth of life insurance. That's it. I know."

He asked if he could set up an appointment for the two of us to go and see an attorney friend of his. I agreed, and we met with the attorney. The attorney asked me all the same questions about my father-in-law's net worth and how much money he had for estate taxes.

I told him everything, and he said, "Well, I'm going to tell you: at his death, he's going to owe the IRS about $85,000."

In today's money, that's about $850,000. I about fell out!

He said, "Let me tell you the problem with that. If he owns 50% of your Burger Kings, whenever he dies, whether you've got one store or five stores or 10 stores, that will be put into his net worth, and there will be even more money to pay. And he's only got $10,000 worth of life insurance."

Man, I tell you, a cold sweat came over me.

The lawyer looked at me, and he said, "I'm going to give you my advice."

You know what? I didn't pay a dime for this advice. I just bought the life insurance, standard rate term life insurance, but I got some great advice.

He said, "I'd go back to my father-in-law and ask him to

Mr. Roy Harris, Murry's father-in-law, standing under the Burger King sign at store #163. He believed in Murry and gave him a chance to own his own business, a goal he had from age 8.

lend you the full $40,000 dollars. You'll pay him interest on it, and you'll be a good boy and take care of his daughter. You'll do all kinds of good things for him, but let you own all of the stock."

I thought, man alive, he doesn't know my father-in-law!

My father-in-law was a great father-in-law, a great man, but I'd already talked him into $20,000, then $40,000. Now I had to talk him out of owning any of the stock.

So Marilyn and I drove up to talk to Marilyn's mom and dad again, and this time, I was asking to borrow a total of $40,000 with no partnership. (That was just the franchise fee; I hadn't even thought to ask for any operating funds. Later, I wound up having to borrow another $2,500 from Marilyn's father in order to have some beginning operating funds.)

I talked to him about it, and he said okay. He was a great man.

And so, I had it all. Praise the Lord! That's all I could say.

Many people hear the story of my success and think everything was easy for me. That's not true—as you can see, I had adversity three or four times before the first store even opened.

What did I do? I didn't give up. I loved Burger King, so I kept working at it. You have to do the same thing. If it were easy, everyone would do it. Then there would be no value in it.

In 1967, I had my third store under construction: store number 373. Mr. and Mrs. Harris had come by to visit us in Mobile, Alabama. They had arrived that afternoon, and I took Mr. Harris to the two stores that were operating. Then I took him to the third store that was under construction. The steel framing was going up at the time.

I pulled up in the car and turned the engine off. He looked at me, and he said, "Murry, you're going to make it."

See, he was wise. He was old enough and had seen enough to know what you need to make it in life. He had a feel for it, and he could understand. He knew I had it.

He said, "Let me tell you something. If you had not gone to The Citadel and made that good record that you did, I would never have lent you that money."

Now he tells me! Do you know what I learned from that? People are watching you.

He'd been watching me since the ninth grade. Of course, Marilyn and I have been in love since we were 14 years old. We went through high school together, and then she went to Florida State University. I went to The Citadel. We got married after I graduated from The Citadel.

People are watching you. You've got to keep that in mind. My father-in-law knew it; the same thing had happened to

The beginning of construction of store #373, Mobile, Alabama, 1967.

POVERTY TO RICHES—MY WAY

The reopening of store #373 after a major renovation and remodeling, January 1992. Marilyn's mother, Mrs. Roy Harris, cuts the ribbon. From left: Murry and Marilyn's daughter, Melinda; their son, Michael; Marilyn; Mrs. Harris; and Murry.

The Burger King crew at the reopening of store #373. Robert Jefferies, General Manager, far right; Roy Gray, District Supervisor, middle of last row.

him. I found out one day when I asked him how he got started in the farming business.

He said, "Well, I didn't have any money. I worked over there where they made clay tile for draining water out of the fields."

He told me about having to walk from where he lived to where he worked. It was about five miles. He walked to work in the morning, and he walked home at night. On his way, he walked past a particular farm on the corner, and he'd always speak to the farmer who owned it as he passed. This went on for several years.

One day, the farmer stopped him. He said, "Roy, I've decided to sell my farm and move to Florida and retire. I'd like to sell it to you."

Mr. Harris said, "I don't have any money."

The farmer said, "That's okay. I'll just sell it to you on credit. You can pay me so much every year when you get the crops in."

Mr. Harris said, "Well, I don't have any money. I don't have any equipment."

He said, "That's okay. I'll sell you mine."

Mr. Harris said, "But I don't have any money."

He said, "That's okay. You just pay me a little bit each year when you get the crops in."

Mr. Harris said, "But I don't have any horses." (Back then, they had to use horses.)

He said, "That's all right. I'll sell you mine."

Mr. Harris said, "But I don't have any money."

He said, "That's okay. I'll sell them to you on credit. You just pay me a little bit when you get the crops in."

POVERTY TO RICHES—MY WAY

Finally, Mr. Harris looked at the man and asked him, "Well, why in the world would you sell me all of this on credit? I have no money."

The farmer said, "Roy, I've been watching you. You've been coming by here for the last year or two. You've come by in the morning—rain, snow, sleet, hail, doesn't matter. You go back home at night. You don't miss a day's work. I've been watching you. I don't have any trouble selling you this farm and everything I have here on credit."

The farmer had been watching Mr. Harris. Later, Mr. Harris watched me. He watched me in high school. He watched me in college, and he told me that if I hadn't made that good record, he would never have lent me that money.

How did I build my business? I used my brains and someone else's hands and money. I used my brains, but I didn't have any money, so I borrowed money from my father-in-law. I invited good people to be on my team, and I used their hands. We all helped each other be very successful.

If you think about it, Burger King also applied this principle. They used their brains, created the concept, and put together the system. Then they sold it to me. They used my hands and my money, and it was very good for both of us.

This principle works. I proved it; now it's your turn to test it.

CHAPTER 6

Location, Location, Location: Choosing the Right City

I had the horse to ride—a business to sell something to the public through. That was Burger King. I had the money, and I had my wife for support and help, a true helpmeet.

Marilyn and I agreed that if this business venture failed, then she would teach school and I would deliver newspapers until the borrowed money and the lease were paid in full. We knew that might mean not having any children, but we were dedicated. We weren't playing store—we were serious.

The next thing we had to settle was which city to work in. At the time, Burger King estimated that it took a population of about 50,000 to support a Burger King. Later on, as fast food became more popular, you could go into cities with much smaller populations, but at that time, you needed a town of 50,000.

We wanted to be in the south, so that's where we started looking. For us, 50,000 people wouldn't be enough, because I didn't just want one store. I had a goal of five Burger Kings, so I needed a town or city of 250,000. Well, Mobile, Alabama, was set at 239,000. I decided that was close enough.

You know what happened? I set my goal too low. Remember, I had nothing—poor boy, no money—so I set a goal of five stores.

When you set goals, in business or in life, don't set your goal too low. What if I'd set my goal at 10 stores instead of five? I might have wound up having over 100 stores!

We ended up choosing Mobile sight unseen. We wrote to the chambers of commerce of about 10 Southern cities with populations around 250,000 or more. We didn't consider Atlanta, Georgia—that market was already taken. We picked 10 other cities, read their materials, and chose Mobile without ever going there.

Mr. Bob Webb, the real estate director for Burger King, went to Mobile on our behalf. He found us a restaurant location and got the owner to agree to build a building for a Burger King restaurant. The cost at that time was approximately $50,000 for the building. The owner leased the land and building to Burger King Corporation, and Burger King Corporation leased it to me.

The payment was $1,124 a month, and I had no money or collateral to guarantee I would pay this lease, just my signature and Marilyn's. I hadn't even had the $40,000 for the franchise license—I borrowed that from my father-in-law.

To set everything up, Burger King Corporation needed my statement of net worth, so they gave me a form to fill out for their files. It was so funny: I filled out the form, and it showed I was worth about $500. I wish I'd kept a copy of that.

Not only that, I went to Jim McLamore with one more thing. When Mr. Harris was going to be 50% owner of the operation, he had to sign the lease. But since he wasn't going to be an owner after all, I went back and said, "Jim, look, could you not require him to sign it? He's 73 years old, and he's not in good health. It'd be best and really take the stress off of him in case I fail and this thing doesn't go."

Jim was a first-class person. He said, "Yeah, no problem, Murry. We will not require his signature."

He took my signature and Marilyn's on the lease. He shouldn't have, as far as a good financial decision—we didn't have anything.

We were worthless, but he took our signatures anyway. Why did he do that?

Well, let me tell you something about business. As you deal with people, you learn to trust your gut feelings. Sometimes, when you make business decisions, that's what you have

The first of 69 Burger King restaurants. This store was opened on October 16, 1963.

to do.

Also, he had been watching me. He tried two or three times to hire me to work for Burger King Corporation. He thought I was made of the right material.

It might not have made sense on paper to lease that building with only my signature and Marilyn's, but in the end, it was a good decision on his part. I paid Burger King Corporation millions and millions in royalties over the next 36 years.

People are watching you. Jim McLamore had been watching me. He gave me a chance in life, as Mr. Harris did. Mr. Harris lent me $40,000 for the first store, and Jim McLamore took my signature on the lease.

On October 16, 1963, we opened for business.

CHAPTER 7

Success Secret #3:
Cause Something to Happen

Once we opened our first store, we were off to a great start. The business did well—it was on track to make money in the first year. I saw that it was going to be a success.

Then, about three months later, McDonald's opened three blocks down the street. Suddenly, we were going broke.

I worked day and night, open to close, from 8:00 a.m. to 11:00 p.m. After three months, I was emotionally and physically drained.

I'd leave the store in the afternoon at 2:30, get home at 3:00, and lie down for a rest, still with my white uniform on. At 4:00, I'd jump up and leave so I'd be back at the store at 4:30. The supper crew came on at 5:00.

Many times, driving back and forth, I cried. I was emotionally exhausted. But I didn't give up. I loved what I was doing, and I was going to be a success.

After two or three months, a Burger King supervisor named Dave Talty came into town. He met with me, and he said, "Murry, I can see you're exhausted. You're working day and night."

I said, "That's right. I've got to make this store work."

He said, "I'm going to give you some advice. You take off one day a week and do nothing. That store will be there the next day."

That was some of the best advice I'd ever been given, to take a day off. Don't work more than six days a week; rest on the seventh day.

A day of rest helped, but it didn't solve the problem: I was going broke, and I owed $40,000. Actually, I owed $42,500, with the $2,500 I had borrowed for operating capital.

I had to come up with a plan to survive. If it was going to be, it was up to me. No one else was going to do it for me.

In the Reserve Officer Training Corps (ROTC) at The Citadel, I learned how to set up a battle plan. It's five steps:

1. Set the goal (what you want to accomplish)

2. Gather the intelligence

3. Draw up the plan

4. Execute the plan

5. Adjust the plan to reach the goal

That's exactly what I did. My plan was to survive. To do that, I needed another store.

My father-in-law had lent me $40,000 to open the first store, so I went back and asked him to guarantee two bank notes for me. I asked him to sign one note for $25,000 at the First National Bank of Mobile, Alabama, and another note for $12,000 at the Van Wert First National Bank in Van Wert, Ohio, where he lived. I needed $45,000, and I borrowed the rest of it from my suppliers.

You may be wondering how I convinced my suppliers to lend me the rest of the money. I'll tell you the truth: I just didn't pay them! I don't recommend doing it this way, but I have to tell it like it is. That's how I did it.

I did pay all of my suppliers eventually. Within six to eight months, I was caught up with all of them. I got them current, and I stayed with those suppliers as long as they stayed in business, until the day I sold. I stayed faithful to them because they had helped me.

Once I had the money for the second store, I called Burger King. Bob Webb, the real estate director, flew into Mobile and found a location. He talked to the real estate agent, John Roberts, who talked to the man who owned the site, Cliff Harris.

Mr. Harris and his wife came to the Burger King that I was operating in Crichton. They looked around, went through the books, and checked everything out. The next day, he called John Roberts and told him he didn't want to build the Burger King for me.

This was a big obstacle. I needed him to build the Burger King; I couldn't afford to do it myself.

Opening a fast food restaurant takes a lot of money. You have three large capital costs: equipment, land, and building. Today, a fast food restaurant building, including the land, could easily cost $500,000 to $700,000. Once you have the land and building, you still need to purchase the restaurant equipment, which can amount to $200,000 to $300,000 per location.

The cost for the land and building is so large that most fast food operators have to lease the land and building from an investor or landowner. That was certainly true when I was trying to open my second store: I could only come up with the funds needed for the equipment and franchise fee.

That's why I had to convince Mr. Cliff Harris and his wife that I was a worthy risk. By building me a Burger King building on their commercial lot and leasing the lot and building to me on a long-term lease, they would be making an investment that would benefit them financially in the long run.

All of my first eight stores were leased—land and building. Once I had opened eight successful stores, I had sufficient cash flow and financial net worth that banks were eager to lend me money to finance the land and building for each new store. I financed them over a 15-year period.

Of course, it was a huge advantage to purchase the land and building, rather than leasing, even though I had to finance it. If I bought the land and building, they belonged to me at the end of 15 years. If I leased the land and building from the landlord, at the end of 15 years, they still belonged to the landlord. But in the beginning, the only way I could afford to open a store was to lease the land and building.

When John Roberts told me Mr. Harris didn't want to build a Burger King and lease it to me, I knew I had to talk to Mr. Harris, so I asked for his telephone number. I called Mr. Harris and asked him if I could come by and visit with him and his wife after the supper shift at Burger King. I got there

POVERTY TO RICHES—MY WAY

about 8:00, and I was there for three hours.

I talked about myself, my goals, what I had done in life, who I was, and what I wanted to do. I wanted to be a success. They told me they enjoyed spending the evening with me, and they'd let me know the next day whether they'd build my Burger King.

I went home and prayed about it, and the next day, Mr. Harris called and told me that he and his wife had decided to build the Burger King after all. So he built that Burger King for me, and I opened my second store on November 22, 1964.

I was counting on the second store to turn things around, but sales were very weak at the new store, too. I was losing my shirt again, only now it was in two stores, not just one.

As the fellow said, "I was so broke, I couldn't afford to go bankrupt." I owed $42,500 to my father-in-law for the first store. I owed another $45,000 for the second store. That's $87,500, which is like $875,000 today. I owed close to $1 mil-

Murry's second Burger King restaurant—the store that put Murry on the road to financial success.

lion in today's money.

I needed something, someone to start connecting those dots, where time and chance take over. And the Lord did.

One Tuesday morning around 10 a.m., just as I was leaving the house to go check on my stores for lunch, the phone rang. It was Hardie, the manager of my second store—the one near downtown.

He said, "Help! We have a line of customers out our front door and all the way to the street. And then, it extends down the sidewalk. Come help us!"

As it turned out, it was Mardi Gras Day. Mobile, Alabama, has a huge carnival downtown for Mardi Gras, just like in New Orleans, Louisiana. On Mardi Gras Day, parades run at least once an hour, from 9 a.m. until 7 p.m. The streets are packed with revelers, and my Burger King was a block from the parade route.

It was an awesome sight, and it continued all day long. We had to borrow supplies from the other Burger King store. Cups, mayonnaise, hamburger meat, hamburger buns, lettuce, tomatoes, onions, pickles, Coke syrup, milkshake mix—you name it, we had to borrow it from the other store.

We also had to ask team members from the other Burger King to come down and help us take care of our customers. It was a fantastic and unforgettable experience for me and for my team.

That day was the beginning of an unbelievably successful career, building my empire of 69 Burger King restaurants. It was the turning point of my business life, and I will always remember it with gratitude.

The Lord intervened and connected the dots for me, and

it continued beyond Mardi Gras. Once people discovered my Burger King, they kept coming back for lunch. I started doing a tremendous lunch trade, and in fast food, lunch is when you make your money.

I had overcome adversity again, and now I was making money. I made something happen.

I overcame adversity many times throughout my 36 years with Burger King. That's how business is: you run into problems, and you have to find a way to overcome them. Many people imagine that once you get your business off the ground, you're home free, but I almost went bankrupt again in 1991.

This time, I needed a little over $3 million to get current on all of my monthly bills. How did that happen? Let me explain.

From about 1984 to 1990, there was massive expansion in fast food. Bankers were lending money to anyone with a warm body to open fast food restaurants, because it was so easy to make money in fast food at the time. While I was building stores, so was everyone else, in all segments of fast food—chicken, burgers, Mexican, pizza, subs, yogurt, you name it.

With so much fast food competition entering the marketplace, my sales began to drop. As sales dropped, my positive cash flow began to drop each year.

Finally, for about three years in a row, my company had a negative cash flow. By 1991, I was in a negative cash position. I needed to borrow $3.3 million to get current on everything.

Then, all of a sudden, money got tight. The banks stopped lending money out, and I couldn't get a loan for the money I needed.

I had to come up with a solution, so I met with Ted Burke,

Pete Portella, and Richard Dukes. Ted Burke was president and chief executive officer of Midtown Restaurants Corporation, my main corporation. Pete Portella was a certified public accountant and my chief financial officer at Midtown Restaurants Corporation. Richard Dukes was a certified public accountant and a partner in the accounting firm of Smith, Dukes & Buckalew. He was in charge of doing the external audits on our books to ensure that all of our numbers were true and correct.

The four of us got together to figure out how we could come up with the $3.3 million we needed to keep the business running.

Richard Dukes said, "Listen, you guys have enough cash flow. If you can just get a loan, you can make it. But if you can't get a loan, you'll have to file for Chapter 11."

Chapter 11 bankruptcy doesn't mean you go out of business; it's reorganization. Still, you have to go through a bankruptcy court and deal with a bankruptcy judge. Richard Dukes told us it would be a lot of problems and troubles.

We didn't want to go that way if we didn't have to, but we had already tried to borrow the money. None of the lending institutions that we had been using would lend it to us. We had tried many times, but all the banks and lending institutions said no.

We were nearly out of options, but Pete Portella said, "Look, I'm talking to General Electric Credit Corporation. Give me one more chance with them. I'm trying to get the representative to see that we do have cash flow to service the debt on a $3.3 million loan. Give me a little more time to work on that."

POVERTY TO RICHES—MY WAY

We agreed to let him try. This was our last shot—if it didn't work out, we'd have to meet again to discuss Chapter 11.

Pete Portella got to work. He ended up leading the General Electric Credit Corporation (GECC) representative step by step through all of our audited financials. At the time, we had about 50 stores and a bunch of different corporations, and he guided the representative through all of it, showing him what was there and what the cash flow actually was. He showed the representative that we had the cash flow to service a $3.3 million dollar loan over five years.

Finally, the guy said, "I see it. Okay, I'll approve the loan."

We got the loan, approximately $3.3 million with a payout over five years. We paid a higher interest rate than a bank would charge, but no banks would lend us the money. If we had not obtained this loan from GECC, we would have been forced into bankruptcy.

Good people make things happen, and Pete Portella made something happen. GECC was our only hope, and they came through for us.

Adversity struck over and over throughout my career, and I had to overcome it. You'll run into adversity in your business, too. That's how life works.

Most people are scared of adversity—think back to the business students I spoke to in Kuala Lumpur, and how terrified they were of adversity. When adversity strikes, you'd better be in the business that you love doing, so you'll have a better chance of surviving.

My high school football coach taught us that you have to be willing to pay the price. Success requires a price—are you willing to pay that price? Are you willing to make something happen? Or will you just throw in the towel and go bankrupt when adversity strikes?

No matter what I do, I want to be the best. I love playing tennis doubles, and before I start a match, I'll tell you, I'm playing to win. I have a winning heart and a winning attitude. It's the same in business: my plan is make something happen so that I can win.

I showed my team my vision to be the best fast food hamburger restaurant chain. Not the biggest—I told them getting big would take care of itself. We just wanted to be the best.

Life is a choice, and which way you go will be your choice. You can throw in the towel, or you can work at it and make something happen. You can come up with a battle plan to solve the problem so that you can succeed.

I once saw a bumper sticker that said, "Life is a beach." No, life is a choice. You make good choices, and you make bad choices. My question to you is, what will your choice be when adversity strikes?

I guarantee you: adversity will come. You will have problems as you operate a business. I had problems for 36 years. You never stop having problems; you always have some adversity. You just have to learn how to handle it. You have to make something happen.

I've set the example for you to follow. I've shown you how I've done it. I made something happen in my business; it's up to you to make something happen in yours.

Here's a quote from the *Wall Street Journal,* titled "Make Something Happen."

POVERTY TO RICHES—MY WAY

You come out of a meeting and someone asks, "What happened?"

And you answer, "Nothing."

You sit in the legislative gallery and someone sits down beside you and asks, "What's happening?"

And you say, "Nothing."

Maybe that meeting room and that gallery should have had the same sign hanging on their walls that, so the story goes, a college football coach pasted in his teams' lockers: "Cause something to happen."

He believed that if you didn't make something happen with a good block, your runners would go nowhere, and if you didn't tackle, the other team would run all over you.

He sure caused something to happen. He won more than 300 games, Coach Paul "Bear" Bryant.

Coach Bryant was the most outstanding American college football coach in the history of the game. He coached the University of Alabama football team to four national championships over his career. He was head football coach at the University of Alabama from 1958 to 1982.

He taught his players to make something happen on the football field, and it's the same in business. When times are tough, you've got to make something happen. When times are good, continue to make something happen, and have fun at it, too.

I've found that you'll run into three types of people in life. There are people who make things happen. They have to make something happen—it's in their nature. Then there are the people who watch something happen. They stand on the sidelines. And then there are the people who stand there and ask, "What's happening?"

Which group are you a member of? I pray that you'll be a member of the Make Something Happen group. If you're going to be in business for yourself, I guarantee you, you have to make something happen. In good times and bad, you have to make something happen.

Murry and Marilyn at the Manatee County High School Jamboree. Marilyn was crowned queen in 1956, their senior year.

THE MACOHI, WEDNESDAY, OCTOBER 19, 1955

HAVE 'HIDDEN' TALENTS

Future Plans For Seniors Include Teacher, Millionaire

A car pulls up in the drive way; laughing voices are heard and there are steps on the porch; then in walk two figures. They both call out "hellos" and the first sits down on the couch. The other, one of those "every hungry" boys, goes straight to the kitchen to "see if he can find some food." These happen to be two well known seniors, Marilyn Lou Harris and Murry James Evans.

Marilyn proceeds to tell something about herself. She says that she was born in Scott, Ohio, on January 24, 1938, moving from there to Bradenton at the age of seven. Murry was born only 11 days later, but just outside of Palmetto, which is about one thousand miles away from Scott, Ohio.

A candidate for the Spring Festival Queen in the eighth grade of Bradenton Junior High, Marilyn reigned as queen in the ninth. In high school she was elected as a candidate for Jamboree Queen in her sophomore and junior years. Murry, returning from the kitchen and serving glasses of orange juice he had just made, stated that he had escorted Marilyn at all these affairs.

Worked During Summer

Murry, the boy with the deep blue eyes and the flat top haircut, worked in Punta Gorda this summer. His plans for the future are rather indefinite, but will probably include one of the following: "become a millionaire, save money and become a dairyman, join some branch of the armed services, or attend college and major in physical education."

Marilyn, who loves to travel and journeyed to Rhode Island with the Exchange group last year, said that besides being in Ohio this summer, she also went to visit her Exchange partner. Marilyn's plans after graduation include attending Florida State University in Tallahassee and majoring in some form of education.

Have Nicknames

"Buck" and "Martie," as these seniors are sometimes called, especially by their families, are officers of the senior class; he is serving as vice president and she as secretary. They both also hold offices in the "M" Club; he is president and she is treasurer. At all the football games you will see these two, since Murry is a member of the football team, while Marilyn marches with the drill squad.

Marilyn is a member of the National Honor Society and represents her homeroom in student council, this being her third year. She was just recently elected secretary of the same organization. Murry, who happened at that time to be dressed in the traditional blue jeans and tee shirt, stated that he is a member of the Key Club.

Win Contests

These two seniors have what you might call "hidden talents." Five foot four Marilyn stated that when she was in the third grade, she won third place in a contest to look most like Shirley Temple. Murry, crunching the ice in his glass after having finished all the orange juice, exclaimed that he had won the best acting award at a church party this summer. He and another girl acted out a skit in which there was only enough money for one of them to go to college and they had to decide which one was to receive this money. Murry proved that he needed the money more and won a toy kiddy car as a prize.

Murry and Marilyn, featured as seniors, in an article from their high school newspaper, *The Macohi*.

The text reads:

Future Plans for Seniors Include Teacher, Millionaire

A car pulls up in the drive way; laughing voices are heard and there are steps on the porch; then in walk two figures. They both call out "hellos" and the first sits down on the couch. The other, one of those "every hungry" [sic] boys, goes straight to the kitchen to "see if he can find some food." These happen to be two well known seniors, Marilyn Lou Harris and Murry James Evans.

Marilyn proceeds to tell something about herself. She says that she was born in Scott, Ohio.

A candidate for the Spring Festival Queen in the eighth grade of Bradenton Junior

High, Marilyn reigned as queen in the ninth. In high school she was elected as a candidate for Jamboree Queen in her sophomore and junior years. Murry, returning from the kitchen and serving glasses of orange juice he had just made, stated that he had escorted Marilyn at all these affairs.

Worked During Summer

Murry, the boy with the deep blue eyes and the flat top haircut, worked in Punta Gorda this summer. His plans for the future are rather indefinite, but will probably include one of the following: "become a millionaire, save money and become a dairyman, join some branch of the armed services, or attend college and major in physical education."

Marilyn, who loves to travel and journeyed to Rhode Island with the Exchange group last year, said that besides being in Ohio this summer, she also went to visit her Exchange partner. Marilyn's plans after graduation include attending Florida State University in Tallahassee and majoring in some form of education.

Have Nicknames

"Buck" and "Marty," [corrected from Martie in the original] as these seniors are sometimes called, especially by their families, are officers of the senior class; he is serving as vice president and she as secretary. They both also hold offices in the "M" Club; he is president and she is treasurer. At all the football games you will see these two, since Murry is a member of the football team, while Marilyn marches with the drill squad.

Marilyn is a member of the National Honor Society and represents her homeroom in student council, this being her third year. She was just recently elected secretary of the same organization. Murry, who happened at that time to be dressed in the traditional blue jeans and tee shirt, stated that he is a member of the Key Club.

Win Contests

These two seniors have what you might call "hidden talents." Five foot four Marilyn stated that when she was in third grade, she won third place in a contest to look most like Shirley Temple. Murry, crunching the ice in his glass after having finished all the orange juice, exclaimed that he had won the best acting award at a church party this summer. He and another girl acted out a skit in which there was only enough money for one of them to go to college and they had to decide which one was to receive this money. Murry proved that he needed the money more and won a toy kiddy car as a prize.

Murry and Marilyn at Easter 1960—another picture of my beautiful helpmeet.

CHAPTER 8

The Foundation of any Successful Business:

Building a Great Team

A great team is the key to business success. Since teams are made of people, it's crucial to understand how people work so you can build a great team.

This sounds pretty basic, but it's a fact: people don't operate like machines. You can't just turn them on in the morning and turn them off at the end of the day. You need to understand what makes people tick. What makes them sad? What motivates them? What makes them lie? What makes them steal? What makes them want to be part of a good team? What makes them want to be bad? You have to understand human nature.

The best book I've ever read on human nature is the Bible. I've spent hundreds of hours reading, studying, and teaching the Bible. As a result, I know a little bit about human nature, especially from Psalms, Proverbs, and Ecclesiastes.

No matter how you learn it, the better you understand

human nature, the better you'll work with your team, the better team you'll have, the more fun you'll have, the more fun they'll have, the more productive they'll be, the more inspired they'll be, and the fewer problems you'll have.

As an entrepreneur, you go into business for yourself, but you're not in business *by* yourself. You're the owner, but you're not alone. If you want to accomplish something and grow your business, you'll need a team. If you're in business by yourself, you're going to be very limited in what you can accomplish.

You will build nothing without a team, and your success will be exactly according to how good your team is. The biggest asset that you will have in your business is people. People make things happen.

On the other side of the coin, your biggest problem is also people. People have health problems. They have personal problems. They have family problems. They have financial problems. They have physical problems. They have emotional ups and downs. That's just people.

What's worse is bad people, or people who have turned sour. They'll start making things go down in your business, so you have to watch.

People make things go up and people make things go down, but you can't build a business without people. You need a good team.

I want to tell you two stories about team members. The first one happened after my first captain left to become a Burger King franchisee. When he left, I didn't have a captain.

I'm not a captain, so I began to look for one. I can do the work of a captain, but that's not my forte. I love putting a team together, seeing the vision, explaining the vision to my team, setting a goal, and then leading the team and showing them what we're going to do. But until I found a new captain, I had to be captain as well as keeper of the vision.

One day, when I was in my office, I got a telephone call. There was a lady crying on the phone. She introduced herself: she was the wife of one of our managers. I knew the manager well, and I had met his wife at some of the company functions—lovely lady. The manager had decided to resign, which was fine. That happens.

I had a head supervisor who was in charge of day-to-day operations since my captain had gone, and she was saying that this supervisor had told her husband he could not get his severance pay for a couple of months, and that he wouldn't get a bonus. There were two or three things that he had told him he wouldn't be getting, and what he did get, it would be down the road at least 30 days.

That infuriated me. I said, "Let me check it out. I'll call you right back."

I left my office and went to talk to this supervisor. I asked, "Is this correct? Did you say these things?"

He said he had, and he tried to give me the reasons why he did it.

I said, "Look, I'm not interested in that. That's not the way you treat people. We don't treat people like that at Midtown Restaurants Corporation."

So I walked into the office manager's office, and I said, "Mellie, would you write a check?" Mellie Parnell was our office manager. Later, Patsy McDonald was our office manager, until I sold. Two great office managers—a very key position on my team.

I gave Mellie the amounts that I got from the supervisor, exactly what was owed to the manager. We wrote the check out to him, and I called the manager's wife back.

I said, "You can come by or send your husband by to pick up a check. It's ready and waiting for you." I apologized to her; I said, "I am very, very sorry that this happened."

You see, I corrected it. When you see something wrong, you correct it.

That's a negative result. I don't like negative results, but sometimes you have to handle them.

Since I was playing the part of captain as well as the keeper of the vision, I ended up going around with this supervisor. I began to observe him.

I found that he was the type of person I called a "grinder." Because of the way he treated people, I learned not to leave him in the stores without me. He was a very talented person, very intelligent, but he lacked people skills.

When he went into a store, he would walk in and speak to the managers. Then, he'd walk around and make a list of things that were wrong. He'd write out a list of eight or 10 things, give them to the manager, and walk out. The manager would be left standing there with his chin down, having been chewed out and given a list of things to correct.

I said, "Man, that's not the way."

As we walked out the door, I would try to leave the manager upbeat. Yes, he had these things to do, but I'd let him know that I appreciated the job he was doing.

I kept looking for a captain, and three months later, I invited this supervisor not to be a member of my team anymore. I'd warned him not to treat people like this, but he wouldn't change. Some people won't change. Some people, you can't change or help.

I have a second story about team members, but this time, it's about a positive result involving my brother, W.T., and a good friend of mine named Sam.

As we developed and opened new stores, W.T. was in charge of ordering the equipment and overseeing the installation in the new stores.

Sam had been working with me for about twelve years. He was in charge of overseeing the construction of the new stores: working with the contractor on building the building and coordinating between the contractor and our company.

Both of them were good men and did a great job in what they were assigned to do, but I got word by the grapevine that W.T. and Sam had been arguing. They had been yelling at one another on the job, and they were talking about getting into a fight.

I thought it would blow over, but a month or two later, the same report came back to me again: they were arguing.

I didn't allow that in my company, so I called them in. I sat them down in my office in front of my desk, and I asked them if what I had heard was correct.

They said, "Yes."

I said, "Well, let me tell you. I'm going to explain it to you very simply: I don't operate like that, and you're not going to operate like that as a member of my team. The next time I hear about the two of you wanting to argue on the job or wanting to fight, which is ridiculous—childish!—be sure that when that happens, both of you just come immediately to the office, because I will write you your last check from Midtown Restaurants Corporation and you will not be a member of my team anymore."

You might say, "Wait a minute, that was your brother. Would you fire your brother?"

Absolutely, in a New York second. In my business, I made business decisions, not emotional decisions.

But you know what the good news is? They knew I was serious, and they heeded my warning. They changed.

There was no more arguing or talk about fighting. My brother finally retired from Midtown Restaurants Corporation around 1996. Sam stayed until about 1992, when he became a franchisee of Signs Now Corporation, another

W.T. Evans and his wife Mary at Midtown Restaurants Corporation's 25th Anniversary celebration.

company I owned. He opened a franchise in Biloxi, Mississippi.

As I said, you must understand human nature. If you don't, you'll have a tougher time managing your team.

I've found that human nature is the same everywhere. I don't care if you're in South America, North America, Europe, Asia—it doesn't matter. You need to find out what makes people tick.

I'm going to give you some guidelines that I used in building my team. They're not in order of significance or importance—they're all important. With these guidelines, I hope and pray that you might be able to pick up some nuggets that you can use in building your team.

Finding people for your team

As you start to put together your team, you may wonder how I found my good team members. One way was simple: I watched people.

Always watch people, and be on the lookout for good ones. When you're out shopping, look at employees in shops. Watch how they're taking care of customers, how they're smiling at them, and how they're waiting on them. Is there a sense of urgency?

When Sam Walton went public with Wal-Mart, he didn't have enough trained managers. He needed good people, so he personally went to Kmart stores to look around and see how they were managed. At the stores that were run well, he would try to hire the Kmart manager to work for him. He did hire many of them.

MURRY J. EVANS

I never did that, although I did hire some McDonald's managers and Hardee's managers when they came and asked to work for me. But the best way to find people is just by watching people.

That's how I found my first captain, Tom Ballinger. I met him at church, and I watched how he ran the Royal Crown Cola Bottling Company in Mobile, Alabama. I knew he was the guy, but he left Mobile to go up to Roanoke, Virginia, to work in a Dr. Pepper plant.

About a year later, I started making some money, and I knew I wanted him to work with me, so I flew up and talked to him.

He said, "Let me pray about it. I'll let you know tomorrow."

The next day, he called and said he'd take the job.

Tom became vice president and general manager of Midtown Restaurants Corporation, and my first captain. He did

Hardie Cazalas, store supervisor, and Tom Ballinger, vice president and general manager of Midtown Restaurants Corporation.

a tremendous job. I had two stores when he joined me, and together, we built up to 20 stores. Then he wanted to become a franchisee himself, so he moved to Oklahoma City, Oklahoma, and bought five stores from the Burger King Corporation.

Tom was a great captain, and I found him by watching people. To this day, as I go into a mall or a shop, I still watch people.

Another way to find good people for your team is to talk to the good people who are already on your team. Let them know you need someone, and ask if they know anyone who would like a good job.

You'd be surprised. Good people bring you good people. Mediocre people bring you mediocre people, and bad people bring you bad people. That's the way it works, so talk to your good people.

For instance, Tom Ballinger recommended Hardie Cazalas, who managed my second store. He was my chief trainer and Vice President of "Handle it." If I had a problem that needed to be dealt with, he would handle it properly. He was with me 17 years; then he became a Burger King franchisee.

My good friend who sold me insurance, Jug Adams, recommended Ted Burke, who became my captain after Tom left. Ted had done an outstanding job with Xerox before he joined me. He came on when we had 20 stores, and together, we built up to 69 stores. He stayed with me until we sold in 1999.

It's worth taking the time to find good people for your team—they're the key to your success.

Great Captains

As you put together your team, pay special attention to finding a great captain.

What does it take to make a great captain? Captains are natural leaders. They lead by example.

Captains can make decisions. A captain can draw up a plan to reach a goal, execute it, and accomplish it. A good captain is fair and has a sense of humor.

Captains watch the numbers on the profit and loss statements. They keep their teams focused. They make business decisions, not emotional decisions. They have the ability to

Murry presenting Ted Burke, President and CEO of Midtown Restaurants Corporation, with his 5-year pin from Midtown Restaurants Corporation.

Marilyn and Murry with Dewey and Helen Eason at a high school class party.

correct and motivate.

Captains can make things happen. They can build a team. They can work with a team to accomplish goals. It's a pleasure working with a good captain.

I've had the pleasure of working with four outstanding captains in my life. The first one was Tom Ballinger, who joined me when I had two stores and helped me build up to 20. The second was Ted Burke, who joined me when I had 20 stores and helped me build the company up to 69 stores before we sold.

The third captain was Dewey Eason. He worked with me and became CEO and President of Signs Now Corporation when we had about 75 franchise stores. By the time he retired in 1998, he had built it up to over 300.

My own son, Mark, is the fourth captain. I still have the pleasure of working with him today.

I didn't realize Mark was a captain until I observed him building a business and working with people. When you're around a kid, you don't always know if he's got any talent or not. You think he has, but you're not sure because he's never been put under fire. Mark fits right in with the other three captains—outstanding.

Hiring and Firing

To build your team, you'll need to hire good people. Before you decide to hire, interview potential team members and pay attention to what they're like.

If they're not a good fit, don't hire them, because they're not likely to change. People seldom change their character. Who they are when you hire them is who they're going to be on your team, so try to hire good ones.

Don't waste your time trying to change people. If you

Mark Evans and Dewey Eason on the company prop-jet plane leaving on a business trip.

coach them and teach them and train them, and you can see that they're not going to fit in, invite them not to be on your team. If you let them stay, neither of you will be happy.

On the other hand, if you determine to ask someone to leave your team, find a replacement first.

One night, I walked into one of my stores around 9:00, and I found the night manager there by himself.

I said, "Hey, where's your team? Where are the other three fellows who are supposed to be here?"

He said, "Well, I got angry with two of them and fired them. They were all friends, so the other one quit, too."

I said, "Uh huh. Now you're in here waiting on everybody by yourself."

That late, it wasn't very busy, but he was running here and there, doing it all himself: taking orders, making the sandwiches, and drawing the drinks. I helped him out for the last hour or so until closing time.

I said, "Well, did you learn anything?"

He said, "Yes, sir. I don't fire anybody until I have their replacement."

I said, "You got it!"

Negative Signs

As you build your team, you may be tempted to use a sign to help you find people. Don't do that.

If I go to a shop and see a Help Wanted sign, you know what that tells me? It tells me they don't have a complete team. I probably won't get good service there, because they're not fully staffed. Never put up that kind of sign in your business. In my business, I never put up any type of sign advertising

"Help Wanted," "Under New Management," or any other type of negative sign.

Prodigal managers

People will come and go from your team; that's normal. Sometimes I'd have managers who had been with me for a few years, and they'd start thinking the grass was greener on the other side of the fence. This happened with general managers and assistant managers; they'd resign and leave us.

Often, within three to six months, they were back at our door asking for their jobs back.

I'd welcome them back: "Hey Bill, where have you been? Good to see you. Yeah, we've got a job for you. It's not your old job, but we've got something that I know you'd be happy to do, and you'd do a great job."

Then I'd offer something a step or two down from the job he had when he left. He'd take it, and before long, he'd be back up to where he was.

I found that the managers who left and came back tended to appreciate how nice it was to work at Midtown Restaurants Corporation. Those managers turned out to be some of the best managers I ever had, and they stayed with me long term. They had been out in the cruel world, and they weren't going to try it again.

Pay Increases

As you build your team, you'll have people asking for raises in pay. I learned how to handle this soon after I signed up for my Burger King franchise. I was working in the company stores in Miami, Florida, to learn the business. There were no manuals—it was all just word-of-mouth teaching.

POVERTY TO RICHES—MY WAY

I was in the Coral Way store one afternoon, when the head supervisor, Harry Henry, said, "I've got to meet with Sally today. She wants a pay increase."

I had never had that situation before, so I wanted to know how to handle it. As I was working in the store, I saw him sitting in the dining room, talking with Sally. After they finished talking and she left, I talked to Harry.

I said, "Well, Harry, how much did you have to give her? What did it cost you?"

He gave me some advice. He said, "I was willing to give her an increase of 10 cents an hour, because she was worth that. But what I did, Murry, is I asked her what would make her happy. And she said a nickel. Five cents more an hour would make her happy. I told her, 'You got it.'"

Always ask people what would make them happy. I remembered that in 1983, after Tom Ballinger left, when I was interviewing Ted Burke to be my new captain.

Ted had a job. Good people will usually have a job, and Ted was no exception. He had a good job.

I talked to Ted, and I told him I wanted him to be my captain. I explained the responsibilities, and I said, "Would you like to do that?"

He said, "Yes, I would love the challenge."

I said, "Well, what would make you happy? How much salary do you want?"

And he said, "Well, I'd like to have $50,000 a year."

I said, "You got it."

I don't know if I ever told Ted this before; if he reads this book, he'll find it out. I was willing to give him $100,000. I needed a good man, and I knew he was a good man. He'd been highly recommended by another man for whom I had great respect.

I knew that Ted was hiring in at a lower price. He didn't want to ask too much, and I appreciate where he was coming from.

I knew what type of person he was, though. Once that was confirmed, I started moving him up. I got him up to $100,000 as soon as I could. Then I got him over $100,000 as soon as I could, too, because he was a good man. Good people make you money; bad people cost you money.

More importantly, I appreciated him. People don't want to be overpaid; they want to be appreciated.

The importance of attitude

As you build your team, choose people with good attitudes. Attitude is even more important than ability. I've always said, "If you give me a person with a good attitude, I'll make a winner out of him. If someone has a bad attitude, I don't care how much ability he has, I can't make him a winner."

I had a friend in Mobile, Alabama, who was on the University of Alabama football team. He was on scholarship, but the coach wouldn't let him play in the regular season games. He wanted to know why.

He went to the coach, Coach Paul "Bear" Bryant, and said, "I came out number one on the all the rankings in spring training. Why won't you let me start?"

Coach Bryant looked at him and said, "You have a bad attitude. Until you change that attitude, you're not going to play." So he got mad and quit.

When he told me about this later, he said, "You know

what, Mr. Evans? Coach Bryant was 100% correct. I did have a bad attitude."

I appreciate someone telling the truth like that. His attitude had obviously improved, or he wouldn't have been able to make that observation or admit it to me.

Work to make your team successful

To have a great team, you need to work toward your team's success. Some people say, "I've got to get out there. I've got to be successful." No, what you want to do is work to make your *team* successful.

Start by training them. If you give them the best training, they'll gain confidence in what they're doing, they'll take pride in their work, and they'll make you successful. Your success is a by-product of their success. Make sure they're successful first, and you'll be successful.

Coach Paul "Bear" Bryant, the football coach at the University of Alabama for many years, was very, very successful. He once said he always looked for the best players. He trained them, and then he let them play. That's how you want to run your team. My team worked with me, not for me. There's a difference.

Once, my good friend Dewey Eason and I went with his wife, Helen, and my wife, Marilyn, to a class party of our high school classmates in Bradenton, Florida.

One of the other party guests had been a year ahead of us in school. He became a banker. We were talking, and he said, "Dewey works for you at Signs Now Corporation?"

Dewey was President and CEO of Signs Now Corporation. I owned the company, but he was the captain. He ran it for me.

I said, "No, he doesn't work for me. He works *with* me." He didn't understand, so I repeated it to him again.

I said, "No, Dewey doesn't work for me. Dewey works *with* me."

He gave me that deer-in-the-headlights look, and I'm sure to this day he still doesn't understand what I told him. Dewey worked with me, not for me. I worked with my team… they didn't work for me.

More guidelines for team-building

Here are some more recommendations for working with people and building a good team.

- **Say no to yes-people.** Don't hire people who only tell you what you want to hear. You want people who will tell you the truth. Then you can make decisions to correct any problems you might have.

- **Never miss a payroll.** Always pay your people on time, every time. That may seem pretty basic, but some people have to be told.

- **Promote from within first.** If you've got job openings, always try to promote from within first. Then your people know they have a chance to move up. When we hired supervisors or general managers, we always looked first at the people we had on staff and could promote.

- **Hire and fire slowly.** I heard one man say, "Hire slowly and fire quickly." He's wrong.

Everybody has positives and negatives. You know the negatives of your present team member. You don't know the negatives of the person you may hire, so it's best to fire slowly.

First, try to work out the negatives with your present team member. If you can't, *then* invite them not to be a member of the team and replace them.

- **Dance with the one who brought you to the dance.** That means taking care of your team members. Good people will make you money; take care of them.

- **Always pay 10% more than the going wage rate in the area.** You want the best, and once you get them, you want to keep them. Paying a little more keeps the wolf from their doors. That's what they want: they want to be able to pay their bills, and they want to be part of a great team.

- **Get rid of bad apples.** Bad people with bad attitudes will cost you money—you want to get them off your team as quickly as possible.

Sometimes a team member will turn sour. When that happens, your team will be watching to see what you do. You have to remove the bad apple from your team. Otherwise, they'll destroy your team. This can be hard, but you have to make decisions based on business, not emotions.

- **The way you treat your team members is the way they will treat your customers.** Think about the way you want your customers to be treated. Are you treating your team members the same way? You need to treat your team members with respect and courtesy, the same way you would want to be treated.

- **Loyalty is royalty.** I taught my team to be loyal to Midtown Restaurants Corporation. I told them, "If you take care of the company, the company will take care of you. If you don't take care of the company, the company can't take care of you."

- **Invite people to be on your team.** Be picky. Invite only the best to join you, and invite people to leave if necessary. I learned that from Norm Brinker, who developed the Chili's restaurant chain and Brinker International.

- **You need a Vice President of "Handle it."** That's a person who can handle things for you. Hire someone like that as soon as you can afford to. You're going to need someone to handle things and solve problems for you.

My wife and I lived in Kuala Lumpur, Malaysia, for six years, and in the first six months, I'd already found two people who would fit the bill. A little later, I found two more. I told Marilyn about the guys, and I said if I started a company in Kuala Lumpur, these guys are the ones I'd hire.

You're always looking for good people, and you need a Vice President of "Handle it."

- **Only expect what you inspect to get done.** Be in your stores; show your team you care about them and your company. George Washington once said that the best fertilizer for a farm is the owner's shadow. I agree with that. Whether it's a farm or your business, the owner has to be there. It won't grow without you there working on it.

- **Hire smart people.** Another thing I learned from Coach Paul "Bear" Bryant is to hire people who are smarter and more talented than you.

  Most people won't do that—their ego prevents them. They're afraid to be around anybody smarter than they, for fear of losing their job.

  You won't lose your job. Actually, you'll get promoted, because that smart person will help you do a good job. Coach Bryant said, "You're only as good as the people you surround yourself with." I agree with that 100%.

Building an enduring team

You build a solid team over time. It's an ongoing process, with people constantly joining and leaving your team.

In a business, you have hourly team members and salaried team members. The salaried people—your manager and office staff—stay with you long term. If you treat people right, you'll have very little turnover there.

With hourly team members, you'll have more of a turnover. We had an average turnover of 300% a year with our hourly team members.

As people come and go, you need to keep building a great team. This starts with giving your team members credit whenever they do something good.

When they do something bad, you take the blame. Accept that it's your fault: you didn't train them properly. If you had trained them better, they wouldn't have made that mistake.

This is another bit of wisdom from Coach Paul "Bear" Bryant. On his team, if the players did something good, they did it. Coach Bryant didn't take any of the credit. And if a player made a mistake, which you'd see many times on the film, he would never blame the player. Although the player actually made the mistake, he would say, "I should have done a better job coaching."

He was right. He was the coach—it was his responsibility to coach the players not to make those kinds of mistakes. And if a good player did something good, Coach Bryant would not take the credit. He'd give the credit to the player. He understood human nature.

I operated my team the same way. I appreciated my team. I let them know I appreciated them, and if they made a mistake, it was my fault. I had to do a better job of training them. It was my job to help them succeed.

I recently received an email from a former team member who had visited my blog at murryjevans.com. This sweet note, sent from her heart, was an awesome blessing to my wife and me. I wanted to share it with you so you could receive a real blessing from a real person.

POVERTY TO RICHES—MY WAY

Date: May 2, 2013 12:49:15 PM CDT
To: info@murryjevans.com
Subject: Contact from BETTYE

Hello, Mr. & Mrs. Evans....

It was so wonderful to run across your blog. It has been years since I have seen you and your wife but I will never forget the kindness you showed me when I was a young teenager working for you at the 2959 Springhill Ave. Burger king. I met and married my husband there and we are still together—35 years.

You never had to make a "show of force" to prove your power as the owner. Your kindness and love of your fellow man led people to know you were the one in control. We talk of you and your wife often, with kindness. You sent me to Texas on your jet once to train employees at a new store. You gave me words of wisdom that have always stuck with me and my husband. I see that your light is still shining bright. I hope this note finds you and your whole family well.

Bettye White
Mobile, AL

As I worked with my team, I tried every day to motivate, inspire, and challenge them to be the best. There have been people in my life who have inspired me to persevere and not to give up. I tried to do the same thing with my team.

With this book, I hope to inspire you, motivate you, and challenge you. I pray the comments and guidelines in this chapter will be beneficial to you as you build your team, on the road to success.

CHAPTER 9

When the Experts are Wrong:

Buying a Pig in a Poke and Making Millions

In the beginning of my Burger King career, after I put down the deposit for my first franchise, I stayed in Miami, Florida, to train and work in the stores. One afternoon, I went to Jim McLamore's office to speak with him about something.

Jim was one of the founders of Burger King. He asked me to sit down, because he had something important to tell me.

He said, "Listen, I want you to understand. In the restaurant business, there are three very important things."

So I took out my piece of paper and my pencil, which was my habit. I always carried a pencil and paper and made notes, so I wouldn't forget things and I'd make sure I handled everything.

Jim said, "The first thing that you must remember when operating a restaurant is location." I wrote down "Location."

He let me write it down, and then he looked at me and

said, "The next very important thing in operating a restaurant is location." So I wrote "Location." I thought, where is this leading?

And he said, "The third one is location."

He reeled me in, just like a fish. It's location, location, location.

He was totally correct. You can have the best concept, the best restaurant, and the best food. You can have the best everything you can think of, but if you have the wrong location, you could very easily go broke. Or you can have mediocre service, mediocre product, mediocre whatever—if you have a great location, you'll be successful and make money hand over fist.

I ran into this recently in Kuala Lumpur. I was there with my friend, Dr. Rahim, to do some consulting work for a very wealthy lady. She had opened a restaurant in a mall, and it was her baby.

It was first class: it really was. She did it right, there's no

Marilyn, Murry, Melinda, and Mark at the grand opening of their Burger King store #1198. This was the fifth store in Mobile, Alabama.

question about it, but she was losing money.

We went to her restaurant and had dinner with her and one of her friends and Dr. Rahim's wife. We talked about the restaurant and what she had done with it, her goals and what she'd like to do, and all of her dreams.

What happened is, she got trapped. She just wanted to make it a success, so she kept putting money into it.

Well, the problem was she had a terrible location. She had a great chef. She had great food and great service. The decor, the fixtures—everything was first class. It was just the wrong location.

Location, location, location! As I built my business, I always remembered that.

As I mentioned, when I chose Mobile, Alabama, for my first store, they had 239,000 people. The Burger King Corporation told me we needed a population of 50,000 to support a store, and I wanted five stores, so I needed 250,000. I thought 239,000 was close enough, so I chose Mobile.

We opened our first store, Store 129, in 1963. We opened Store 163 in 1964. In 1968, we opened Store 373. In 1972, we opened Store 1089, and in 1973, we opened Store 1198.

Tom Ballinger joined me when I had two stores, and he helped me build up the additional three stores. So I had the five stores I wanted, and we were doing well.

We had just bought a little old house and set up our offices in it, very basic. I actually didn't have an office there—it was just a small house—but Tom had an office there.

One Tuesday, I was sitting in Tom's office, and he said, "Murry, we need to put a store at the University of Alabama in Tuscaloosa."

I said, "The University of Alabama in Tuscaloosa? I know there's a store there already. I know the guy. His name is Leonard Jacobs."

How I knew Leonard Jacobs is another example of time and chance, or connecting the dots. Almost 10 years earlier, my wife and I had been in Cherokee, North Carolina, on our way to Ohio to visit her parents. We were in a line of traffic, waiting for a parade to pass in downtown Cherokee, when a fellow behind me hit the back of my car. He just rolled into it—boom!

I got out, and he got out. He was a good southern boy, and he said, "Man, I'm sorry."

I said, "Hey, no problem."

I looked at my bumper, and there was just a little dent in it. I said, "Don't worry about it. I'll handle that when I get home."

He said, "Oh, where are you from?"

I said, "Mobile."

He said, "Man, I'm from Tuscaloosa."

I said, "Tuscaloosa? You have a Burger King there?"

He said, "Yeah, you know, we've got a Burger King there."

He told me where it was, and when I got back in the car, I said to Marilyn, "Hey, this is a real nice guy. We're going to go back through Tuscaloosa."

Normally, we never went through Tuscaloosa, Alabama, coming from Ohio back to Mobile. We always went through Birmingham, Alabama.

This time, we went through Tuscaloosa, and I went to the Burger King and met the owner, Mr. Leonard Jacobs. He was a super gentleman.

I looked at his store, and it was very basic. It was not really a Burger King; it just had the name. He was selling soup to nuts. He was doing a good job with what he had.

We talked, and I told him what I was doing. At the time, I had two stores, and he said he'd come down one day to see me. A few months later, he did. He came down and spent the day with me around the stores. I gave him some advice and helped him as much as I could.

That was around 1965 or 1966, and we didn't talk again until 1972. That Tuesday, I got the telephone number for the Burger King in Tuscaloosa, and I called him.

I said, "Leonard, this is Murry Evans down in Mobile."

He said, "Yeah man, where have you been?"

I said, "Man, I've been busy. Listen, I want to know, would ya'll be interested in selling your store there?"

He said, "Yes, we certainly would. We're talking about that."

I said, "Well, good. I'll be up there tomorrow morning about 8:30 at the airport."

He said, "Okay. I'll have my friend, Paul Caldwell, pick you up."

Paul Caldwell was one of the three owners; the other two were Leonard Jacobs and D.O. McClusky.

Paul picked me up at the airport and we drove around Tuscaloosa, and I asked him, "Well, what do you want, Paul?"

He said, "Well, we want $120,000, and we want 6% interest on it, but we'll finance all of it, nothing down for six years."

I said, "Okay."

He said, "By the way, there was a man here from Montgomery on Monday, a Burger King man. He looked at buying our store, but he said $120,000 was too much, so he left."

I didn't know that—see, time and chance. He visited the store on Monday. Tuesday, I called. Wednesday morning, I flew up in my airplane. I had a professional pilot fly with me in case of weather or other problems, and I got there early.

I looked at this thing, and I said, "Hmm. It's not how much it costs. The important thing is, what is the true value?"

That requires vision. You have to look at something and be able to see its value in the future and what can be done with it.

I saw value in this property, so I wanted to sign a letter of intent. A letter of intent is a non-binding letter specifying your agreement on what you intend to do. We put in there what we wanted to do, the sales price, and the terms. They agreed, and I typed up the letter with the understanding that I'd be back the next morning with my wife, who was secretary of the corporation and had to sign, and my attorney.

I flew back to Mobile, and we got up early the next morning. I got Sam McMillen, my attorney; Marilyn, my wife; and Jim Vaughn, the pilot; we all flew up on Thursday morning. We worked out the legal work and got it all typed up and signed. Jim Vaughn was the witness to it. We shook hands and went back to Mobile on Thursday.

So I called on Tuesday, and I owned it on Thursday. How did I do it so quickly? I did it with an airplane.

I saw that it was of value, because what I bought was the name "Burger King." This was totally separate from the Burger King Corporation in Miami. In Tuscaloosa County, Alabama, D.O. McClusky, Paul Caldwell, and Leonard Jacobs owned the rights to the name "Burger King."

Now, I couldn't use the Burger King Corporation's particular colors or logo for this store, but I still had the name Burger King, Home of the Whopper. I wanted to open up more regular Burger Kings, but most importantly, I wanted the opportunity to control Tuscaloosa County. That's what I was really buying.

We signed the deal, and the next day around noon, I talked to Leonard again.

He said, "Hey, let me tell you what happened. The man from Montgomery returned this morning and said 'Okay I'm ready to buy. I'm ready to pay you the $120,000.'

"I told him, 'We don't own it anymore. We sold it.'

"And he said, 'You sold it?'

"I said, 'Yeah, we sold it yesterday.'

"He said, 'Who did you sell it to?'

"I said, 'We sold it to Murry Evans.'"

Leonard said the man was very, very angry.

You might say that was just coincidence—another coincidence happened in my life that just put me in the right place at the right time. No, it's not coincidence. It's time and chance. You can call it connecting the dots if you want to, but I call it time and chance.

So, what happened next? Well, I owned the rights to Tuscaloosa, but I couldn't open a standard-looking Burger King. I understood that, so I called Burger King.

They knew I had bought it—the word got out—so I went down to Miami, Florida, to meet with the region vice president, Jerry Winter.

He told me that I would not open any more franchises

with Burger King Corporation, the standard Burger King as you understand it today. He said as long as I owned the name Burger King in Tuscaloosa County, Alabama, they would not let me open any more franchises.

I didn't want to be a renegade. I just wanted to work in the system, but he was trying to get me to understand that I had wasted my money.

He said, "Murry, I think you just bought a pig in a poke."

I said, "Okay. That's okay."

Do you know what a pig in a poke is? In the late Middle Ages in England, people would sell a piglet in a poke or a sack. You'd go to the market to buy a piglet, and the guy would pick it up and put it in the sack and hand it to you.

Well, if you weren't watching, he might pick up that sack and put in a rabbit, or a puppy, or a cat instead of your piglet. He'd hand it to you, and you'd walk away. The term was "buying a pig in a poke." It meant you'd better check and make sure

Murry and Marilyn in front of their store #1380, Tuscaloosa, Alabama.

POVERTY TO RICHES—MY WAY

that what you have in the poke or the sack is of value.

Jerry Winter was basically telling me I had bought something of no value. I thought to myself, Nah, I don't think so.

I negotiated the best deal I could. What I did was swap the rights to the name "Burger King, Home of the Whopper" in Tuscaloosa County. I swapped that to Burger King Corporation for two franchise fees.

At that time, the franchise fee (not including equipment or anything like that, just the franchise fee) was $36,000. By swapping for two franchise fees, I got $72,000 in return for the rights to the name "Burger King, Home of the Whopper" in Tuscaloosa County, Alabama.

Now, let me tell you about that pig in a poke. When I sold, 27 years later in 1999, the pig in a poke had grown to six stores. They were very, very profitable—the most profitable segment of stores I had. Those six stores represented 20% of my bottom line.

What does that say about the experts? The experts were wrong.

You've got to always watch experts. They're wrong at least half the time, if not more.

After I bought that pig in a poke, I immediately built a second store in Tuscaloosa, by the interstate, and it began to climb in sales and profits. Within 10 years, it produced a yearly bottom-line profit of over $400,000.

I also remodeled the first store, and it just began to print money. After I bought that pig in a poke in Tuscaloosa, I was always looking to buy another pig in a poke.

* * *

For my next site, I wanted to go to Laurel, Mississippi. I'd heard that the McDonald's there was doing extremely well: sales around $1.4 to 1.5 million, which was huge at the time.

I called Burger King, and I got the okay to go ahead and build a store. I started looking for a location in Laurel, which is about 100 miles from Mobile.

I went to Laurel and met with the Burger King real estate representative. We looked around, and there were really only two pieces of property available, both owned by Pennzoil. The best piece of property was even better than the McDonald's location. It was the first location coming off the interstate.

When the real estate representative found out it was owned by Pennzoil, an oil company, he said, "You can forget it. They never sell property. They only buy property and land bank it."

In other words, like putting money in a bank, they put land in a bank. They call it a land bank, and then they use the

Burger King #1465 under construction in Laurel, Mississippi. Standing beside the Burger King sign, from left: Mark, Melinda, and Marilyn.

land whenever they get ready to build a service station on it.

I said, "I don't know about that." I kept at it—I made something happen. The Pennzoil Company's headquarters was in Houston, Texas, so I started making telephone calls.

I finally got in touch with the real estate representative who was responsible for Mississippi. I talked to him, and he was a nice man. I explained who I was and what I wanted to do.

He said, "Well, I don't know. We've had it a long time. I don't know whether they have any plans to do that. I'll tell you what we can do. You give me what you want to do with it, and we'll present it to the board and see whether they want to sell it. And if they do, they'll tell you what they want for it."

I didn't know what they were going to ask for it; it was a great site.

I waited at least six months, maybe a year. You know how fast a big corporation moves? It moves kind of like an elephant—very slowly—or sometimes like a snail. I kept calling him, and he'd say, "Well, they're going to meet." And then, "They're going to meet." And, "They're going to meet."

Finally, I got a call from him, and he said, "Murry, let me tell you. They met. They said they would sell it for $145,000." Of course, that was a lot of money at that time.

I said, "Okay, I'll pay it." I did, and that became one of the most profitable stores I ever had. Just because someone tells you something can't be done—in this case, purchasing land from an oil company—it doesn't mean you can't make it happen anyway with a little bit of determination.

* * *

The next site I developed was in Tyler, Texas. I wanted an interstate site—there was an interstate going through the north part of Tyler. I already had two stores in Tyler, and I wanted two more.

I had a site on the west side of town, and I wanted to put one up on the north side, where I-40 went through. There was a McDonald's there, and I knew what they were doing in sales. They were doing terrific.

I found a piece of property, and I found the owner. I said, "Look, I'd like to come out and visit with you."

He was just an old country boy, and he said, "I'd be glad to, Murry. We get off about 5:00 on Friday afternoon, if you could come by my office."

He told me where it was, and he said, "About 5:30, I'd be glad to sit down and talk with you."

It was a great piece of property, so I got in my Lear jet and flew out there. A friend of mine, Phil Hardy, went with me, and we met with the owner in his office. We sat down with him and talked about the site, and he said, "What do you want to do?"

I said, "I want to put a Burger King on it."

He said, "Okay."

I said, "Well, would you like to sell it?"

I knew I was dealing with a country boy. When you're dealing with a country boy, you've got to watch him. Country boys will deal with you straight, but they can be tricky, too. They can negotiate you right out of your front teeth if you don't watch them.

This guy was good—he wouldn't trick you. He was straight, just a good solid businessman.

He looked at me, and he said, "You know, my brother and I bought that site about, I don't know, three years ago. We were going to move our nursery business out there on it, but we've talked about it, and we have agreed to sell it. We paid $50,000 for it, and we've agreed to sell it if you'll pay us $100,000."

My teeth about fell out of my mouth. I looked at my friend, Phil. On the way out there, he had asked me what I'd pay for the site. I told him, "This is an interstate site. Interstate sites are always the highest-volume fast food sites. I'm prepared to pay $200,000 to $250,000 for this site. It'll be worth it." And it would have been.

When the man said, "If you'll give us $100,000, we'll sell it," I couldn't even talk. I was speechless; I just couldn't answer the man. I looked at Phil.

Phil spoke up and said, "Murry, man, that's a lot of money." He broke the ice.

I said, "Yeah, you're right, Phil. But you know what? I'll go ahead and pay it." I looked at the man, and I said, "I'll take your offer."

We shook hands on it, drew up the papers over the next week or two, and I bought that piece of property for $100,000.

I learned, always let the other person mention price first. I let him mention price first, and he said, "I will be happy if you will give me $100,000." It was just like the hourly girl who wanted a raise with Harry Henry down in Miami. She was happy with a nickel when he would have given her a dime—twice as much. I was willing to give this man more than twice as much, but he was happy and I was very happy.

***

The next site I want to tell you about is Spanish Fort. Spanish Fort is in Baldwin County, Alabama, on the east side of the Mobile Bay. The interstate goes right by there—I-10 going to Mobile. I pulled up there, and there was a McDonald's and something else, maybe a chicken place, and several gas stations.

I knew the McDonald's was doing extremely well, and I was looking to put a store in that area. There was a prime spot open, the first site coming off the interstate, but it had a big Exxon sign on it: "Exxon, Coming Soon." Exxon had done their work well—that was the number-one site at that intersection.

I pulled in there, and I went to the convenience store and gas station right next to this empty Exxon lot. I went in and talked to the owner. He was an Alabama country boy from up in the north of Alabama. We started talking, and I told him who I was and what I wanted to do.

I said, "Man, I'm looking for a site. I'd really like to have this site right next to you, but I see they're going to build an Exxon there."

He said, "No, they're not going to build an Exxon store."

I said, "They're not? That's what the sign says. They're going to build an Exxon gas station and convenience store."

He said, "No. Two years ago I bought this land right here from Exxon, and in my agreement I have a non-compete. They cannot sell oil and gas over on that site. I had that put in, and they didn't realize it. They thought they could sell this to me and also sell oil and gas. They cannot. My attorney has stopped them."

I said, "Wow."

Again, time and chance. Nobody knew that, did they? But I found it out by going and talking to folks.

I called up Margie Baxter, my real estate broker, who handled things for me. She was a bird dog: I'll tell you—she would flat handle things.

I said, "Margie, I want to buy this Exxon site." I told her the story on it.

She said, "I'll jump right on it."

We got on it, and we bought it. We paid a hefty price—we paid $325,000 for that piece of property—but it just made money hand over fist. And isn't that why you're in business, to make as much money as possible?

* * *

Another site I want to tell you about is store number 2483 in Mobile, Alabama. It was out on Airport Boulevard. I had one store on Airport Boulevard closer to the interstate, but out toward the airport, there was no fast food.

I looked at it, and I drove all around it, back in the back roads and back streets. I even had a traffic counter, like highway and traffic departments use. You put it out and leave it 24 hours, and it counts the cars as people drive over it. We used that to find out exactly what kind of traffic we'd have in a given location.

We did that on this site, and I got in my airplane and flew all around it, looking at it, looking at all the homes, looking at the traffic movement and everything. I saw the development that was going on, and I said, "That's a great site."

I called Burger King and told them I wanted to put up a store in West Mobile—another store in Mobile.

They said, "Good, we'll send the real estate rep out."

He came out and looked at it, and I could tell he didn't like it. I explained to him why I liked it, but he still didn't like it.

He said, "Murry, I don't really like it, but I'll okay it for you."

I said, "Okay, great. I appreciate it."

After the store opened, my franchise district manager told me, "Murry, I want to tell you something. The real estate rep said that this store was not going to do anything. He said it wouldn't make money for two or three years, but Murry has a lot of money, so let him go ahead and open up the store. It'll be good, and it'll grow into it, and he'll make some money after two or three years."

The first year, I "only" made $225,000 bottom line, pre-tax. I made something happen.

There will always be those who doubt your decisions, but in the words of the American frontiersman and politician David Crockett, "Be always sure you're right—then go ahead." You've got to get your own gut feeling about a business.

* * *

The next site, and the last one I'll tell you about, is Vicksburg, Mississippi.

Ralph Herring walked into my office. He was Director of Operations in Midtown, and he said, "Murry, we need to put up a Burger King in Vicksburg."

Vicksburg was about 40 miles from Jackson, Mississippi, and we already had three or four stores in Jackson.

I said, "Yeah, that'd be great."

POVERTY TO RICHES—MY WAY

He told me what the McDonald's was doing—he'd found out from the bread man how much McDonald's was doing, and they were minting money. So I said, "Okay, let me jump on that."

I called the Burger King real estate rep. It was a lady who had this area that we were interested in, and I called her and said, "Hey, is anything going on in Vicksburg? I want to apply for a franchise for Vicksburg."

She said, "Well, Murry, to tell you the truth, we're already working on a site there, and we're going to make it a lease."

I didn't want to hear "Burger King lease," because that's leasing a property—in 20 years, you don't own any property. If you buy it, like I was doing at all of my sites, you own the land and building plus the business at the end of 20 years. You had more value by owning the property.

I said, "Well, look, could I fly down to Miami and buy your lunch?"

She said, "Yeah, no problem."

So I got in my plane again. Out of these six sites, this is the third site where I used my plane. If I hadn't had it for the site in Tuscaloosa, Alabama, I might not have gotten the site at all.

That plane made me money. Was it expensive? Absolutely. Does it take money to make money? Absolutely. Are you willing to spend money to make money? You'd better be.

For the site in Vicksburg, I flew down to talk to the real estate rep. She was a very nice lady and very efficient. She knew her business.

I talked to her, and I said, "Let me ask you something. Do you have a franchisee set up for this yet?"

She said, "No."

I said, "I want to be the franchisee."

She said, "I'm sure that's no problem. We'll check with Operations."

She did, and Operations said, "Yeah, Murry can have Vicksburg."

I said, "Let me do this. If you let me go ahead and buy that property instead of Burger King buying it and leasing it to me, in six months to a year I will put up another store in Vicksburg."

She said, "Let me think about this."

She thought about it, and we kept having lunch and talking about business. Finally, at the end of the lunch, she said, "Okay. I'll okay you taking it over and buying that property and owning that property yourself."

I said, "Well, praise the Lord."

Marilyn, her mother Ireta Harris, and Murry preparing to leave to visit their Burger King stores.

Again, I used my airplane. I made something happen.

Vicksburg was an interstate site. It was an awesome site. I opened that site in 1983, and we had unbelievable business. We set a record: we did over $66,000 in the first seven days. That was a worldwide company record for Burger King at that time, and we didn't do anything, we just opened the store. We didn't take out newspaper ads or TV ads or anything saying the store was open. We just opened it up.

It was tremendous, and it made us money year after year. It was a great location.

Interstate sites always produce higher volumes and more profit. Near an interstate, you have two areas from which to get business: the population living around your store, and the transient interstate traffic that would stop to buy gas and get something to eat. Having a combination of the nearby residents plus the interstate traffic creates higher volumes, which create higher profits.

This was one of many times when I used my airplane. To me, it was an indispensable tool. It made me money. It was expensive, but it didn't cost me money, it made me money.

It's the same with a car: it's expensive, but it makes you money. You can drive around in it and go to different sites. If you really want to save money, you can sell your car and just walk. You'll really save, but you have to watch saving money. It's not "saving money to make more money." The program is to increase sales and control costs to make more money.

You can save yourself out of business. Did you know that?

Once, there was a man who had a hot dog stand. He sold all-beef hot dogs, and he had billboards out, and he had signs all over his site. It was a simple old building, and he just sold hot dogs and root beer.

He didn't have a college education. He didn't even have a high school education, but he had a good product, and he had a good location and a good price. He had billboards all around town, and he was just selling the daylights out of those hot dogs.

He made so much money, he sent his son off to college. When his son came home from college, he said, "Dad, do you understand that the country's in a recession?"

He said, "No, I didn't."

And his son said, "Well, it is. You need to cut back some of these expenses. You need to cancel some of these billboards, because things are tough."

He said, "Oh, I didn't realize that."

His son said, "Well, I recommend you canceling those billboards out there on the outside of town."

So he did, and sure enough, business did drop. His son came back a little bit later, home from school, and he told his dad, "See, I told you it was going down. You need to get rid of the rest of these billboards to save that money."

So he said, "Yeah, I guess I'd better do that."

So he did, and sure enough, sales dropped some more.

His son said, "I want to tell you something else, Dad. You're selling an all-beef hot dog here. You need to put some chicken and pork in that and maybe some binders, some soy binder in there to cut that cost so you can make more money."

He said, "Yeah, I'll do that." So he lowered the quality of his hot dog.

The next thing you know, his son was right. The country was in a recession, and people were going out of business, and he went out of business.

What happened? He saved himself out of business. Don't let that happen to you.

* * *

You may be thinking about location, location, location, and wondering how you can choose a good site. I'll tell you, there are many ways.

I used to take census tracts. (This was before Google Maps.) I also used a traffic counter to take traffic counts.

I wanted to check and make sure that the people could get in and out of the site easily. I also talked to businesses in the area. I wanted to know how they were doing, how their sales were and how they had done two years before and last year—was it growing?

You learn what you can, and you get a gut feel for the location. Then you make the decision.

For the rest of my Burger King career, I kept building stores and expanding, always looking for another pig in a poke.

I had a captain in charge of operations—running the store once it was built—and I was responsible for finding the sites, negotiating, finding the financing, and supervising the construction. Our deal was that I'd build them, and my captain would run them. Tom Ballinger was my first captain, and I did the same thing with Ted Burke, my second captain.

With them running the stores, I was free to keep building more stores. It worked great, and we had fun, building stores and making more money.

The second of 69 Burger King restaurants that Murry developed and owned.

Murry and Marilyn with a dining room poster from 1965. This poster was presented to Murry and Marilyn at their 25th Burger King anniversary celebration by Mr. Fred Wessel, Burger King franchisee in Huntsville, Alabama.

Midtown Restaurants Corporation's office building, Mobile, Alabama.

Mark with corporate Learjet, ready to return to Mobile, Alabama, after visiting Midtown Restaurants Burger King stores in Florida.

Murry and Marilyn in the Signs Now booth at a large franchise expo.

CHAPTER 10

The Genius of Execution:

Getting the Most out of People Smarter than You

One of the best things I ever did for my business was to join a group of like-minded franchisees who wanted to exchange ideas, support each other, and make our businesses the best they could be.

This group was called the Licensee Educational Group—LEG Group for short. David Stein formed it in 1975. He was the Burger King franchisee for the area around Jacksonville, Florida. He didn't feel he was getting enough support from the Burger King Corporation, so he formed this group.

The corporation couldn't come close to the kind of support we got from each other, meeting with sharp, like-minded franchisees who wanted to run top-notch businesses. I was invited to the third meeting, and I was in the group from 1975 to 1999, when I sold.

The LEG Group was made up of people who made things happen. You're only as good as the people you surround yourself with, and in this group, I surrounded myself with people who made things happen.

A lot of people do similar things: meet with other people in the same business by joining clubs or associations, or by going to business conferences, conventions, or seminars. Some people call it networking. I call it hanging around people smarter than you.

Remember, Coach Paul "Bear" Bryant said, "Always hire people smarter than yourself." He said, "I always hire assistant coaches who are smarter than me."

In tennis, if you always play against players weaker than

Mr. Jules Lederer, founder of Budget Rent-A-Car Corporation, speaking at the 25th Anniversary celebration of Midtown Restaurants Corporation. I hired Mr. Lederer to be a consultant to me for my Signs Now Corporation and my Burger King operations. I learned from a man smarter than me.

yourself, you will never improve your game. To improve in anything in life, you must be around people smarter and better than yourself.

In the LEG Group, we weren't really networking. We were just meeting with other people who were doing the same thing and had our money and time invested in the same concept—Burger King. We were meeting in order that we could run a better and more profitable operation.

The LEG Group was composed of 20 members. It was by invitation only, and I received my invitation from David Stein himself. He sent me a letter inviting me to come to the next meeting, which was held at Camelback, in Phoenix, Arizona, in 1975.

I'm so thankful he invited me. The LEG Group was one of the biggest factors that helped my business career. The members were great operators, and I grew from the information and ideas we exchanged.

In 1978, David had invited Norm Brinker to come and speak to us in Atlanta, Georgia. Norm Brinker founded Steak and Ale; he also owned and developed the Chili's restaurant chain and founded Brinker International. It was a tremendous opportunity to hear what he had to say.

At the time, he was working for Pillsbury. He was the one who talked with Don Smith, one of the top operating vice presidents at McDonald's, and got him to come to be president of Burger King Corporation.

I had a chance to talk to Norm Brinker personally at lunch when we were in Atlanta. We had a one-day meeting with him that included lunch. I was sitting at a table with Jim Drury and Chuck Keidel, and Norm asked to join us. He did, and we had a tremendous time talking with him.

And as a result of that, when I needed some advice about 10 years later, I called him up. I needed some advice on what direction I was going with my company and business.

He said he'd be glad to talk with me. He asked me to come around 5:30, after he closed his office and everybody left. We had the office to ourselves, and we probably spent an hour and a half talking about business. He gave me some tremendous information and advice.

* * *

Another way the LEG Group helped us learn and improve was through profile tests. Earlier, I mentioned the profile test about characteristics of your ideal job. On another occasion, they sent us a personality profile test.

One day, as I was walking out of the office, my secretary stopped me. Her name was Debbie Butts.

Debbie said, "Mr. Evans, you need to fill out this personality profile test and send it in for the LEG Group meeting next week."

I said, "Look, I don't have time. You fill it out and send it in."

She said, "No problem," and she did it for me.

At the next LEG Group meeting, the lady went over everybody's tests and her analysis of them. When she got to mine, she said, "Now, everybody's seemed normal except Murry Evans's. Murry Evans's profile test seemed like a woman had filled it out."

Jack Jones, one of the members out of Dallas, spoke up and said, "Murry had his secretary fill that out, I'll bet you."

Of course, everybody broke up laughing.

The lady asked me, "How is this?"

I said, "That's right. I didn't have time to do it."

I made her day. She thought that was the greatest, that I would change and not do what everybody was supposed to do. Everybody else in the group did exactly what they were supposed to do, but I didn't.

As I told you, you can't figure out which hole I go into—a square hole or a round hole—because I don't fit a hole. I march to my own drummer.

I'm a little different. I remember reading something not too long ago that said, "Be different or die." Well, I guarantee you: I am different. I'll make decisions and do whatever is necessary to move along, as long as it doesn't hurt anyone. I had things to do that day that were more important than filling out that profile test, so I had Debbie fill it out.

* * *

In the LEG Group, we brought together all kinds of ideas: operational ideas, financial ideas, playground and building ideas, marketing ideas, advertising ideas, and promotional ideas. We shared all kinds of ideas and information.

It was the greatest group I was ever with. I learned so much, and it really helped grow my business. We talked about equipment, construction bids, team member problems, incentive programs—you name it. Everything you can imagine it takes to run a business, we discussed.

One of the things we discussed was ways to increase sales and control costs to make more money. That's something we learned from Don Smith, president of Burger King (a former vice president of McDonald's). He came and spoke to us, and we asked him, "What's the difference between Burger King and McDonald's?"

He said, "The first thing I found coming into Burger King was that the Burger King corporate staff are trained to get up in the morning and think, 'How can I cut costs to make more money?'

"At McDonald's, we weren't trained that way. We were trained at McDonald's to get up in the morning and think, 'How can we increase sales and *control* costs to make more money?'

"Thinking, 'How can we cut costs to make more money?' will put you out of business shortly. You're going to have costs. You just have to control them to make more money. There's a big difference."

* * *

The LEG Group gave me some of my best marketing ideas. One great idea came from Ed Davis, one of the members out of Pennsylvania. It was the idea of a 100-foot flagpole.

I put a 100-foot flagpole with an American flag in about six or seven sites—interstate sites, where the pole was visible for a mile or two. It was a tremendous marketing tool.

I also got the marketing idea of a 99-cent Whopper from one of the franchisees in the LEG Group. I'll discuss the 99-cent Whopper later, in chapter 13.

At least as valuable as the meetings, we also talked one-on-one over lunch or dinner, on the tennis court, or going shopping. Being able to talk business one-on-one with the other franchisees in the group was very valuable to me.

Remember, you're only as good as the people you surround yourself with. The LEG Group was a tremendous source of ideas to improve the operation and profitability of my stores.

I loved being in the LEG Group. It was an absolute pleasure. If you're in business for yourself, I highly recommend that you get with like-minded people who are in the same industry and learn from each other. Meet with them, go to conferences, attend seminars. Whatever it is, it's money well spent.

One day, after I'd been in the LEG Group about 17 years, I was in the car with David Stein, the founder of the group. By this time, he knew me very well.

We were going to get lunch, and we were talking about business and what deals and developments I was working on at the time.

David looked at me, and he said, "Murry, you are a **real entrepreneur**."

I said, "Well, thank you, David, for those very kind words."

It's true; I just love business. Hearing him say that I was not just an entrepreneur, but a *real* **entrepreneur**, was one of the best compliments I've ever received.

CHAPTER 11

The Danger of Playing it Safe: Burger King's Double Drive-Thru

In 1963, when I started with Burger King, the drive-thru was not a big part of Burger King. When I was in Miami, training in the company stores, I think they had two stores with drive-thru windows.

They had the concept, but the buildings weren't laid out properly for it to work well. They actually took the drive-thru windows out of the two stores I worked in, because it just wasn't practical.

The fast food drive-thru was not really perfected until 1970, when Wendy's opened a drive-thru unit that really worked. They got it right. Everyone—Burger King, McDonald's, Taco Bell, KFC—everybody copied Wendy's drive-thru window.

Why was it successful? It was convenient. You stay in your car, so you save time. Remember time and money. People found it very convenient to stay in their cars instead of getting out and going into the store.

For conventional stores that had a full dining room and a drive-thru window, the norm was about 50/50 on sales. This was true back when I was operating, and it's true today: you did about half of your sales at the inside order counter and half on the drive-thru window.

In the 70s, I added a drive-thru window to my existing stores that had dining rooms. Each store increased sales 40 to 50%. I could not believe it. It was an awesome increase, which increased my bottom line tremendously. That gave me the money to continue growing and expanding.

People love drive-thrus. They're convenient, if they're fast. One thing they don't like is sitting in a drive-thru that's not moving. In chapter 14, I'll tell you about an innovation that I added to my drive-thrus to speed up the service tremendously.

Well, if one drive-thru lane is good, imagine what you could do with two. When someone came up with the idea of a store with a double drive-thru lane, that was a no-brainer to me. The choice was obvious.

That's exactly what happened in 1986: a new hamburger company called Checkers opened its first store in Mobile, Alabama, and it had a double drive-thru. They were extremely successful; they now have over 800 double drive-thrus.

When they opened, it was the first double drive-thru I had ever seen. They opened it next to one of my high-volume stores, and it hurt my sales.

I knew I needed to do something about it. I contacted Burger King Corporation, and I said, "Hey, I need some help. Checker's just built a double drive-thru next to one of my stores. It's hurting my sales, and I know they plan to grow and build more. What are we going to do?"

Burger King chose me to work with them and a leading architect and designer, Richard A. Morris, from Fairfield, Ohio. We teamed up to plan, research, design, develop, and open the first franchisee double drive-thru building—a completely new concept to Burger King. This was a downsized building with two drive-thru lanes and a small 16-seat dining room. It required an entirely new design from the ground up.

It became an outstanding success that generated an additional 20% bottom-line profit over conventional stores, so I wanted to take it a step further. I met with the Burger King executives in Miami, Florida, and presented the idea of copying Checkers.

Checkers didn't have a dining room at all. They had a double drive-thru and picnic tables. If you wanted to eat there, you would park your car, go to the window, order, and eat at a picnic table or in your car.

Many people don't realize this, but McDonald's and Burger King both started out with no dining rooms. At the first McDonald's and Burger King stores, you would just park your car, go to the window, order, and sit in your car to eat. Later, they added some picnic tables, and eventually, dining rooms. The first Burger King I ever saw did not have any dining room, just picnic tables.

The advantage of no dining room was lower capital cost, which meant a higher bottom line. It certainly wasn't a new or untested idea—Burger King started out that way. But Burger King Corporation insisted on a 16-seat dining room in the double drive-thru design. They started adding costs to it. That's like taking a racehorse and hitching him up to pull a wagon.

The new buildings were called Double Drive-Thru Zoom Buildings. I opened one store with the original 16-seat design. When I wanted to open two more (one in Gulfport, Mississippi, and one in Tuscaloosa, Alabama), Burger King required that I add 24 seats to the concept. They continued to add costs.

Burger King didn't see the vision that I saw. My idea in business is always copy success. If I see someone else doing something, I don't want to reinvent the wheel. I don't care that it's their idea—as long as it's legal, I'll use it.

My team worked with Burger King Corporation and Richard Morris's team to design, develop, build, and open the first franchise Burger King Zoom Double Drive-Thru store in the world. We opened it in Mobile, Alabama, and it was a complete success.

This building, minus the 16-seat dining room, could have

The first franchised Burger King double drive-thru building, Mobile, Alabama, 1988.

POVERTY TO RICHES—MY WAY

been used by Burger King Corporation to put Burger Kings everywhere.

There was a place for Burger Kings with dining rooms, no question about it. But there were also many, many places where you could have put a double drive-thru with no dining room, and it would have worked extremely well. You could have put these Burger Kings everywhere. The capital cost was so much less, and the operating profit percentage was so much higher. Burger King could have made a run to catch up with McDonald's with this concept.

Mr. Jim McLamore, co-founder of Burger King Corporation, with Marilyn and Murry at the grand opening of their first double drive-thru Burger King restaurant.

Unfortunately, that didn't happen. After several years, the concept was scrapped. I'll give you one reason: lack of vision.

The management became scared. They played it safe.

It's human nature. I understand that. They said, "Well, we'll just do a roofed building with a dining room. We've always done it this way." No, they hadn't always done it that way. I remember when Burger King had no dining room.

To succeed in business, you have to be different. The decision to build a Zoom building with no dining room was a no-brainer, as far as I was concerned. Checkers proved the public wanted the concept. Burger King's corporate management was just too scared to do it.

McDonald's made the same mistake. They tested several buildings. I visited one in Detroit, Michigan, and I remember standing there looking at it and thinking, "Man, I hope they don't build these everywhere. We'll really be in trouble if they develop this."

They could have, but they didn't. Just like Burger King, they both chose the safe route.

The two largest burger companies in the world made the same mistake. That is why you don't see Burger King and McDonald's double drive-thrus everywhere across the landscape.

Murry and Marilyn inside their Burger King store #1380 in Tuscaloosa, Alabama.

CHAPTER 12

Five-Cent Jelly:

How Hardee's Unwittingly Helped Me Add Breakfast

One day, around 1982, I was going to my Burger King corporate office in Mobile, Alabama. Along the way, I stopped at a Hardee's to buy a couple of sausage biscuits for breakfast. I regularly stopped there to pick up something for breakfast on my way to the office.

I went to Hardee's rather than one of my Burger Kings because, at the time, we didn't offer a breakfast menu. Hardee's unwittingly helped me change that.

Hardee's main breakfast items were biscuit sandwiches, and they were good. Instead of going the easy way and using frozen dough to make their biscuits, Hardee's made the biscuit dough from scratch, combining the individual ingredients and baking them fresh each morning.

You could tell the difference. Those biscuits were better than biscuits made from frozen dough. As far as I was concerned, Hardee's biscuits were the best breakfast item available from fast-food chains at that time.

On this particular day, I went through the Hardee's drive-thru to pick up two sausage biscuits and two packets of strawberry jelly, which had become my standard order. After I gave my order, the cashier said, "That will be five cents extra for each packet of strawberry jelly."

"What?!"

"Sir, it's five cents for each packet of jelly."

I was so irritated by this, I told them to forget it. I drove away without any biscuits or packets of jelly.

What had they done? Instead of making me feel warm and fuzzy all over, they had irritated me, and over only 10 cents. Don't nickel and dime your customers with added fees or tacked-on expenses. It's not worth it.

As I thought about my poor customer experience at Hardee's, I decided to add a breakfast menu at my Burger Kings, with biscuits made from scratch. McDonald's had added breakfast to their stores in the early 1970s with the advent of the Egg McMuffin, and Hardee's had followed suit soon after, but Burger King had been slower to add breakfast to their menu.

Breakfast is the hardest meal to add because breakfast customers tend to go to the same place every time. They're very loyal. I knew it would take a lot of hard work to convince people to switch and start coming to my Burger Kings for breakfast, so I had put off making the change. My stores were doing fine without it, so it hadn't been a pressing matter.

On the other hand, I thought the industry as a whole was moving toward an all-day menu with breakfast included. I decided the sooner I got into it, the better off I would be.

I called Burger King's regional corporate office in Atlanta, Georgia, to get some information. Then I went to visit some of the franchisees who were experimenting with adding breakfast in their stores.

They were making biscuit sandwiches, as I planned to do, but instead of making the dough fresh, they were using frozen biscuit dough. I didn't want to do it that way.

I found a Burger King owner in Beaumont, Texas, who was a former McDonald's franchise supervisor. He was making biscuits from scratch for the breakfast menu in his stores, so I went to visit him. He showed me how breakfast worked in his stores, making the biscuits from scratch, the way I wanted to do it. I learned a lot from him.

When I got home, I ordered the extra equipment necessary to start offering a breakfast menu and, most importantly, making biscuits from scratch. We began offering breakfast, with scratch biscuits as a key part of the menu. People could order biscuit sandwiches, biscuits and jelly, or a platter of biscuits with a white sausage gravy. That was a big seller.

In the beginning, we adjusted our biscuit recipe a few times, until we hit on the right formula. Once we got that, our biscuits were just dynamite. We didn't have to make any more changes after that.

It was tough at first. We started with no sales at breakfast, but we marketed heavily and offered a superior product. Over time, we built up a following of loyal customers. Breakfast eventually became a very profitable part of the day for us, and the fact that we were offering scratch biscuits drove many customers to us.

Looking back, I probably should have written a "Thank

MURRY J. EVANS

You" letter to Hardee's for provoking me into adding breakfast to my Burger Kings. We sold a lot of biscuits, but we never charged extra for jelly.

CHAPTER 13

Brand or Traffic Marketing:

Two of My Most Successful Promotions, and Corporate's Surprising Response

I In business, there are two main types of marketing: traffic marketing and brand marketing.

Traffic marketing is focused on bringing people through the door of your store or to the homepage of your website. The focus is on encouraging the customer to pay you a visit, in the hopes that it will lead to a sale, and hopefully, future sales. Without traffic, there are no sales, and soon, no business.

Brand marketing shifts the focus away from traffic, concentrating instead on promoting your business's image or logo—your brand. I call it "feel-good marketing."

Once you get big enough, you need to participate in brand marketing, but you have to wait for the right time. When you start your business, your entire marketing budget needs to go into traffic marketing.

Traffic marketing has to come first in order to drive people to you, and it has to always continue. Every month, every week, every day, you have to be doing something to build your traffic and bring people to your business. If you stop traffic marketing, you are making plans to go out of business.

Not everyone understands this. In 1989, a British company called Grand Metropolitan (Grand Met for short) took over Burger King. Burger King had previously operated under the umbrella of Pillsbury, but Grand Met completed a hostile takeover of Pillsbury, so Burger King became part of Grand Met.

I was on the Burger King marketing council, and Grand Met sent over a young man to introduce a new marketing program. This young man's program was focused on brand marketing, brand marketing, and more brand marketing.

Not surprisingly, the franchisees rebelled. We had to convince him that we needed to keep doing traffic marketing to stay in business.

I'm not saying brand marketing isn't valuable. Once I got big enough, I did lots of brand marketing. A few things I promoted included a cancer awareness tennis tournament in Mobile, Alabama; the Azalea Trail Run; and a John McEnroe / Vitas Gerulaitis exhibition tennis match.

I promoted these and many others, but only after I had solid cash flow in my marketing budget. Even when I did brand marketing, I never stopped traffic marketing. Brand marketing might not happen every month, but I did traffic marketing daily.

It's the same for your business. You'll eventually need both types of marketing, but initially, you need to focus on traffic marketing. You need to keep that up every day, throughout the life of your business. In time, when you have the extra cash flow to be able to afford it, you can add brand marketing to the mix.

Over 36 years, I used all types of traffic marketing—promotions designed to bring customers in through our front doors or into our drive-thru lanes. The two that were the most effective were "Buy a Whopper, Get a Whopper Free" and the 99-Cent Whopper. Any time I needed to drive traffic to my stores, I would put a coupon for "Buy a Whopper, Get a Whopper Free" in the local newspaper. We call that marketing promotion a BOGO: Buy One, Get One.

We had a lot of success with the BOGO, and around 1980, we took it a step further. A company called World's Finest Chocolate came to us and offered us a marketing proposal for our stores in Mobile, Alabama. They were a national company that worked with schools and other organizations to help them raise funds for whatever projects they might have.

They had a chocolate candy bar that sold to the public for 50 cents, and the selling organization kept a portion of the sales price. They asked us if we would be willing to put a coupon on the label of their chocolate bar, offering "Buy a Whopper, Get a Whopper Free."

We said yes. To us, that was another no-brainer. The community looked at it as Burger King helping the community, and we were. Meanwhile, they helped us by becoming loyal customers long past the initial BOGO coupon. We did it for years. It was enormously successful.

Would you believe Burger King Corporation asked us not to do it?

Every year, they asked us not to do it. They said it degraded Burger King's flagship sandwich, the Whopper.

The World's Finest Chocolate sales representative who had the Mobile market was the number-one World's Finest Chocolate salesman in the country for volume. It was a tremendous promotion. Yet, every year, Burger King said, "Please don't do that again. That's just degrading our flagship Whopper sandwich."

I told Burger King, "Sorry, I can't do that. I will continue to do the promotion. The community loves it, I love it, and World's Finest Chocolate loves it." Everybody loved it except Burger King Corporation.

I couldn't figure out why, because it increased sales, which meant that I put more money into the 4% marketing budget, and I also paid more royalties to Burger King Corporation.

They kept asking me to stop, but I wouldn't. As long as I was responsible for paying the rents and meeting the payroll every two weeks, I was going to continue the promotion. Burger King Corporation wasn't responsible—I was. It was up to me to do what it took to increase sales, in order to increase profits, in order to build new Burger King Stores, in order to send more royalties to Burger King Corporation.

Each month, we paid approximately 3% of that month's sales to Burger King Corporation as royalty fees for using the Burger King name and their system. That was fair; I had no problem with it. I *wanted* to send more royalty fees every year.

A lot of franchisees don't like sending royalty fees, but I didn't mind. If I send more royalties each year, that means I'm doing more sales. Of course I want that!

Burger King Corporation didn't understand that. Remember, large corporations think differently than a struggling entrepreneur with his money and life invested in his own business.

I had to make something happen. That was my goal each day. If I didn't make something happen, the paychecks would stop. I would be out of business. I had a big payroll to meet every two weeks, and there's nothing like having to meet payroll to get you motivated to make something happen.

I stuck with the "Buy a Whopper, Get a Whopper Free" promotions because they were very successful, but there was one promotion that was even better: the 99-cent Whopper. The 99-cent Whopper promotion was the greatest promotion that I ran in my stores during the 36 years I was in Burger King. It contained unbelievable price value, which of course my customers wanted, so it was incredibly popular.

I got this idea from Dennis Hitzman in Phoenix, Arizona. He had developed this promotion at a time when he was going broke and had to make something happen or close his stores.

He made something happen, and it worked. He survived.

I heard about it around 1994, a time when I was struggling, so Ted Burke and I flew out to visit him. He graciously showed Ted and me all of his numbers.

The promotion was very simple: all Whoppers, 99 cents. Of course, a cheese Whopper was 10 cents more. But if you wanted a Whopper, it was 99 cents, and you could buy all you wanted. You didn't have to buy a Whopper and get one free. It was just buy a Whopper, 99 cents.

You want 10 Whoppers? No problem—99 cents each. Twenty Whoppers? All you want.

You could buy a 99-cent Whopper and walk out. You didn't have to buy fries or a drink or anything. But along with the 99-cent Whopper, Dennis had put together nine combos. A combo was a sandwich, french fries, and a Coke.

At this time, combo meals were just beginning to come into the fast food industry. Today, if you go into any fast food restaurant, all you see on the menu are combo meals: chicken, tacos, burgers, pizza— plus fries and a drink. But it wasn't always this way. In the early days of fast food, you ordered individual items a la carte from the menu.

The first year we did this promotion, we gave large fries and large drinks with the combo. After that, we dropped it to medium. We actually had customers say, "I can't eat all these fries; I can't drink all this drink." So we listened to our customers and dropped it to a medium-size fry and a medium-size drink.

Sales kept climbing. The combo had a discounted price, lower than the total if you purchased each item separately, so people loved it.

I had never sold

99-Cent Whopper promotion on a free-standing Burger King pole sign.

99-Cent Whopper promotion on the windows of the Burger King building.

a combo meal in my restaurants before introducing the nine combo meals along with the 99-cent Whopper promotion. But there I was again, in on the beginning of a new innovation in fast food: the combo meal!

I love being on the leading edge of new innovations. That's where the excitement and fun is!

Of course, with the combo and the 99-cent Whopper, food costs went up a few points. But more importantly, sales went through the roof. The first year we tried this, my company, Midtown Restaurants, went from a $500,000 bottom line to a $2 million bottom line, pre-tax. The last year of the promotion, I had a $2.4 million bottom-line pre-tax profit.

I ran this promotion for five years. In those five years, I made over $10 million, bottom-line pre-tax profit.

How did Burger King Corporation react to our 99-cent Whopper promotion? They constantly asked us to stop the promotion. They said it degraded the Whopper, their flagship sandwich. They felt that a flagship item like the Whopper should carry a higher price to set it apart from sandwiches of lesser quality.

They were worried about protecting their brand, but I was the one who had to pay the bills. I wanted a promotion that would generate the highest possible traffic and sales. I was always looking for another pig in a poke, and the 99-cent Whopper was the greatest pig in a poke that I ever found.

Burger King Corporation would never agree with me on this. We may have had our differences, but they never refused the larger royalty checks I was sending as a result of this winning marketing strategy.

In 1999, I knew I was selling my company of 69 stores. Ted Burke, the president of my company, said, "Murry, Burger King is begging us to stop the 99-cent Whopper promotion."

I said, "Okay, do it."

So we stopped the promotion and took all of the signs down. We went back to the standard combo price, no 99-cent Whopper.

Of course, our sales dropped immediately. For the year ending September 30, 1999, our profits dropped to $150,000. That's down from $2.4 million in 1998. In one year, I lost $2,250,000 from the prior year.

Burger King Corporation got what they wanted, but they still purchased my stores based on the profit of $2.4 million in 1998.

Does the customer want price value? You tell me.

CHAPTER 14

How to Make Money:

Add Value and Control Cost

If you have a business, you want it to make more money. Everyone does. That's what business is about. To make more money, all you need to do is follow this simple plan. Each morning, when you get out of bed, think, "What can I do today to increase sales and control costs, to make more money?"

It's really very simple. If you increase sales and control costs, you will make more money.

You don't want to *cut* costs to make more money, because you have to have costs. Costs are built into a business. You want to *control* your costs, and you want to increase sales. If you do both of those things, you will make more money.

A lot of people just focus on increasing sales, but if you increase sales without controlling costs, you will not make more money. You'll do a lot of work for nothing.

This is very simple, so you may be thinking, "That's easy

for you to say!" But even increasing sales is easy.

To increase sales, all you have to do is add value to what you're selling the public. Whether it's a product or a service that you're selling to the public, add value to it. Then, add more value to it. Create value for your customer.

Over the 36 years I was in Burger King as a franchisee, I did many things to increase value for my customers. In this chapter, I will cover two of them, plus one thing I did to control costs.

One way that I increased value for my customers was in the way I fried my french fries. I changed from a short, fat crinkle cut to a long, slim shoestring cut; I changed the oil I was cooking the fries in; and I changed the temperature of the oil.

How did I come to make this change? That's another example of time and chance.

Every day, on my way home, I passed McDonald's. One day, when I was driving past, I looked into the McDonald's parking lot, and I saw a gentleman walk out of the building towards a car parked in the lot. He looked like he might be the owner of the franchise, so I wanted to meet him.

I pulled into the McDonald's parking lot, got out of my car, and introduced myself to the gentleman. I was right: he was the owner of this McDonald's.

That was the beginning of a lifelong friendship. Over the years, we became very close friends. We'd visit each other's stores—he would come down to my store and eat Whoppers, and I would stop by his store and eat french fries.

Why did we do that? Well, he had the best french fry, and I had the best burger.

We always went in the back door when we visited—it was a small community, and we shared a lot of the same customers. We didn't want them to see us going into our competitor's building.

One day, in his store, I began to look at how he cooked his french fries. I saw he used a temperature of 315 degrees, whereas I used a temperature of 365 degrees. Also, he wasn't using vegetable shortening, like I was. He used a beef tallow and cottonseed oil mixture: 82% beef tallow and 18% cottonseed oil. This gave the french fry a delicious flavor.

If you know anything about cooking, flavor comes from fat. Our hamburgers were 80/20: 80% lean, 20% fat. If you didn't have the 20% fat in there, it would be like eating ground-up shoe leather. There would be no flavor at all.

Fat is the key, so I wrote down the name of the company that manufactured McDonald's french fry shortening. It was a company called Interstate Foods, located in Chicago, Illinois. I called them and asked if I could get the same shortening they produced for McDonald's.

I figured the answer would be no, and it was. He said, "No, but I can actually sell you the same product under my label, just a different stabilizer." It was his own brand, and it was called Frial.

Since it wasn't the exact same product, he could continue to sell to McDonald's with no problem. He told me I'd get basically the same flavor from it as the shortening they made for McDonald's.

I ordered ten 50-pound cubes drop-shipped to Mobile, Alabama, and it really was an awesome shortening. I could barely tell the difference between Frial and what McDonald's was using.

I used the new shortening and the lower cooking temperature. I also ordered shoestring french fries from my supplier, Fruit Distributing Company.

Before I put in the new fry procedure, french fry sales had been 14% of total sales. With the new procedure, french fry sales shot up. Suddenly, french fries accounted for 30% of total sales.

As french fry sales went up, profit went through the roof. If you know anything about fast food, you make your money on french fries and drinks. The other food cost is too high. If you just sold burgers, you'd go out of business.

Before, I had a bottom-line pre-tax profit of 20% to 22% of sales. After I put in the new french fry procedure, my bottom-line pre-tax profit became 30% to 32% of sales each month.

It worked because I added value for the customer. I didn't

Murry in front of his second store in 1967.

raise the price of the french fries, I just made them absolutely, awesomely delicious. That gave customers more value. The new french fries increased the traffic to my store, so I sold more burgers and drinks.

I was very happy with the whole thing. The new fries, Simplot shoestring french fries, were absolutely the best french fries in the world. Over the 36 years I was in business, sometimes I'd have to use something besides Simplot, and I guarantee you the quality was not the same as Simplot. Simplot still produces the best french fry anywhere.

Fruit Distributing Company supplied the Simplot shoestring french fries to my stores. One morning, Mr. Nelson Horner, the owner of Fruit Distributing Company, walked into my store with another gentleman, the Simplot representative from Idaho, where the Simplot factory was.

I still had only two stores at the time, but the Simplot representative told me he came from Idaho to Alabama to find out why I was selling twice as many french fries as any other Burger King in the world. Whatever their volume was, I sold twice as many for the same volume.

He wanted to know why, and I gladly showed him. In fact, I was so excited that I called Burger King Corporation in Miami. They sent the franchise district manager to visit and check out what I was doing.

When I showed him the new french fry procedure and the results, I couldn't believe what he said.

He told me to take out the Frial shortening and return to Burger King's cooking specifications. I was floored.

Of course, I was a young man at the time. I was 27 or 28 years old, and I thought people were interested in putting out the best product and making more money. But I was fooled.

I learned something about human nature. People don't want to know a better way to do something. They want you to do it their way.

I couldn't believe they weren't interested in my results. They were only interested in me following their specifications. In other words, don't bother me with the facts—my mind is made up.

I didn't take the Frial out. So, what happened? About three or four months later, the franchise district manager came back and gave me an ultimatum: take the Frial out of your stores, or take your Burger King signs down. Unbelievable, but it's the truth.

I wanted to be with Burger King—I was sold on the Burger King concept—so I had no choice. I took out the Frial. (I did keep the Simplot shoestring french fries.)

However, I was proven correct in my french fry cooking procedure. Ten years later, when Don Smith was hired from McDonald's to be president of Burger King, the first thing that he did was put Frial shortening in all the stores. He lowered the cooking temperature of the fryers to 315 degrees, just like I had done. I was just 10 years ahead of my time.

* * *

The new french fry procedure was an example of adding value to a product. Next, I want to talk about adding value to a service, specifically, the drive-thru service.

I had about six stores that had been built with no drive-thru windows, so when we added that service, we had to build on. We had to bump out the kitchen wall on the side, moving the side wall of the kitchen out to be flush under the roof of the building.

In this bump out, we placed a window, and that's where the drive-thru worker waited on cars, collecting money and delivering food and drinks to our customers.

One day, while observing a lunch period at one of my stores, I noticed there was a car waiting at the drive-thru window, not moving. That got me thinking, and I realized that we could not move the drive-thru line until the front customer had received his or her order.

That may seem obvious, but it was only obvious to me after it hit me in the face. This was the way we had always done it—this was the way drive-thrus operated.

Watching the line not moving, I thought, "We've got to do something. I don't want our customers to be waiting in line. Our customers need to be moving. They want to spend their money with us, not their time."

So I got to thinking about it. I thought, what if we had a door in the drive-thru bump out, facing forward? We could take a customer's money and ask them to move forward. Then, when the order was ready, a team member could run it out to the customer.

So I had doors put in all my drive-thrus, opening forward, toward the street.

When a car arrived at the drive-thru window before their order was ready, we would collect the payment and ask the customer to move forward to wait. We had it clearly marked where they should stop and wait. Then the next car in the line would move up to the window, and we would collect their payment. By then, the order would be ready for the first car that had moved forward, and a team member would run it out to them.

That's how we used the drive-thru door to speed up our drive-thru service, and it was tremendously effective. With the drive-thru door, we added more value to our customers' experience at Burger King, because they didn't have to wait as long. That made them happier, so they would come back again more often.

That's what business is all about: creating more value for your customer on a continual basis.

Did I get Burger King's approval to install doors in the drive-thrus? No, I didn't. It was a no-brainer. It lowered the amount of time my customer spent in the drive-thru, waiting and wasting his time.

I didn't ask Burger King for permission before I did it, for one simple reason: I learned early in life, it's easier to get forgiveness than permission. I figured if

Murry in his office in 1993.

POVERTY TO RICHES—MY WAY

I asked them first, they'd probably say no.

Adding the forward-facing door to the drive-thru was very successful. With the drive-thru door, I could serve more customers in a given time period. If you serve more customers in the same amount of time, you increase sales, and you make your customer happier. That's what you want in business.

Remember, to make money, increase sales and control costs. Also, remember time and money: customers would rather spend their money, not their time. I was always looking for ways to make them happy by saving them time.

After I'd added the door to my drive-thrus and the concept proved successful, I received a call from the vice president of Burger King operations internationally. He was the top vice president of operations. He had heard about my drive-thru door and wanted to visit and see it in operation. I said, "Hey, no problem. Come on."

I picked him up at the airport, and we observed the drive-thru doors in action at several stores.

He didn't like what I had done without his permission, but I proved to him that it increased service for our customers. It'd be a blind man that couldn't see that it worked. But I also remember that when he left, he had a puzzled look on his face.

He didn't tell me to take out the doors, like 10 or 12 years before, when they made me stop using the Frial shortening and my new french fry procedure. Back then, I only had two stores... I was a small fish in the pond.

Now, I was a big fish. I was sending them nearly $1 million in royalty fees each year, with over 25 stores. I was also building more stores on a regular basis. So, they looked the other way and let me continue.

About three months later, I wanted to build another store, so Burger King sent me the current building plans. The new Burger King plans had a door in the drive-thru bump out. Did this mean the vice president of operations had accepted my idea of the drive-thru door? Well... not exactly.

On the plans, they had the door opening to the rear of the drive-thru bump out, not to the front so you could run the orders out to the waiting car.

I don't know why they would make the door open to the back. I don't know whether they were going to take garbage out to the dumpster or what, but he completely missed the purpose of the drive-thru door. Now I know why he had that puzzled look on his face when he left: he had missed the point of what I had done.

I continued to build my drive-thrus with doors that opened forward, so we could provide fast service, adding more value for our customers.

My innovation of adding a door in the drive-thru was the precursor to the two-window drive-thru system that was eventually implemented throughout the fast food industry. Other fast food operators came to the same realization I had: the need to speed up service in the drive-thru. They attacked the problem by installing another window at the rear of the building. The first window would collect the payment for the order, and the second window would deliver the order to the customer. It was a great idea.

In the early 80s, I installed the two-window system in several of my high-volume stores. As I built new stores, I had them built with the two-window system—plus the door. By using all three facets of the drive-thru system, I was able to totally maximize the speed of service in our drive-thru lanes.

Remember, you have to get up every morning and think of how you can increase sales and control costs. Improving the drive-thru is my second story on adding value, which is how you increase sales. Now, I want to tell you a story about controlling costs.

When I started in Burger King, they dispensed mustard and ketchup using plastic squeeze bottles, like the kind you probably have at home in your refrigerator. You squeeze mustard out of them; you squeeze ketchup out of them.

If you were supposed to put mustard and ketchup on a burger, you'd turn the bottle over and squeeze a certain amount—what you thought was the right amount.

One fellow could say, I like a lot of ketchup, and someone else would say, I think a little bit of ketchup is enough. The hamburger would taste different, depending who made it, because it would have different amounts of ketchup and mustard. There was no consistency.

One day, I was in my friend's McDonald's, eating french fries. I looked over and saw him with a stainless steel dispenser, squirting ketchup and mustard on the burgers.

I asked him about it, and he said, "Oh, these are from a company called Prince Castle. You can order them. They're not proprietary to McDonald's—anybody can order these."

It was amazing: you could set the amount of each squirt.

The dispenser was very simple. It held about a quart-size container, and you held it in your hand. You just pushed the lever down one time, and it dispensed the correct amount. Whether you wanted a half ounce, one ounce, an ounce and half, two ounces, whatever—you could set it to dispense the exact amount you wanted on each burger. It was very easy and very controlled.

I thought it was awesome. I immediately went out and ordered some for my Burger Kings, along with a dispenser for tartar sauce for our fish sandwiches. This way, we could control the exact amount of condiments on each sandwich. That meant the flavor of the sandwiches would be consistent: no matter who made them, they would have the same amount of condiments, so they would taste the same.

On top of that, controlling the exact amount of the condiments on each sandwich meant I could control food costs.

You must control costs to make money, and I immediately saw that this was a way to control costs. With the squeeze bottles, the amount of condiments used on each sandwich varied, depending who made the sandwich, so the food costs varied. With these dispensers, it was consistent and controllable.

What was Burger King's reaction? Basically, they had the same reaction as they had to my Frial.

They came in, they looked at what I was doing, and they said, "Take out those Prince Castle portion control dispensers and go back to the squeeze bottles. Or, take your Burger King signs down."

The last time I was in a Burger King, I think they were still using squeeze bottles.

***

I've told you one true story of how I added value to the product that I offered my customers. That was my french fry story: using Frial shortening, lowering the temperature, and using Simplot shoestring potatoes.

POVERTY TO RICHES—MY WAY

I've told you one true story of how I added value to the service that I offered my customers: my drive-thru doors that opened forward so that I could speed up the service for my customers.

I've told you one true story of how I improved cost control and the quality of the flavor of my burgers, by using Prince Castle dispensers for mustard, ketchup, and tartar sauce.

In each case, I've told you the true story of Burger King's reaction.

After reading the true stories of how I attempted to add value and cost control to my stores—and Burger King's reactions—you might think I was very disappointed with Burger King Corporation.

Absolutely not! Let's set the record straight.

In any relationship, there are two sides to the coin and, of course, differing opinions. Burger King Corporation's responsibility was to protect the uniformity of the franchise brand. Over the years, they have done an outstanding job of protecting the brand, system, and concept, along with giving great support to the franchisees. That's one reason the brand is still extremely strong. I am very thankful for that!

My responsibility was to take the franchise system they licensed to me, and build the best franchised hamburger company in the world. By the grace of God, that is what I did, with the help of my team!

Burger King Corporation and I had an awesome 36 years working together to make something happen. And, we did: 69 successful Burger King restaurants.

It was a fantastic ride!

CHAPTER 15

Poverty to Riches:

Selling for Millions

I remember one day in ninth grade, my home room teacher, Miss Warren, asked each of us to write down what we wanted to be in life: a doctor, an engineer, a lawyer, an electrician, whatever it might be. It was good; it made you think.

We did the assignment, and she collected them and started reading over them. She was going through them, making comments. Then she stopped, and I could tell she was reading mine.

I knew what kind of answer she wanted, but I had written that I wanted to be a millionaire. I hadn't decided what I was going to do or be to become a millionaire, but that was my basic goal.

Miss Warren called me up to her desk and explained that she meant a doctor or a lawyer or whatever.

I said, "Yes, okay. I understand." I apologized and told her something—I don't know what—so that she could put something down on the paper.

Then, in the twelfth grade, my future wife and I were interviewed by the school newspaper. Marilyn and I were in the same grade in high school at Manatee County High School in Bradenton, Florida. Our senior year, the school newspaper interviewed us and took pictures of us for the paper.

In the interview, they asked about our goal in life—what did we want to do as a job or career?

Marilyn said she wanted to be a schoolteacher, and I said I wanted to be a millionaire. She reached her goal first—she became a teacher before I became a millionaire.

Everyone asked me why I wanted to be a millionaire. Well, I was poor. A lot of folks have never been poor in their life, but I had been poor since I was born. I was born into a good family; we were just poor. It's not a sin to be poor, but it certainly is a handicap.

By the time I graduated from college, I'd already experienced about 22 years of being poor, and being poor wasn't much fun. I'd had enough of being

Murry and Marilyn, in the living room of her home, in their senior year of high school.

POVERTY TO RICHES—MY WAY

poor; I wanted to try something else.

This book is my story of how I attempted to become a millionaire. Starting out, I didn't know what I wanted to do in order to become a millionaire. To tell you the truth, I had no idea. I just knew that I didn't want to do *poor*.

Being poor motivated me to try something else. If you've never been poor, then you don't understand what I'm talking about.

I knew I wanted to own my own business, and I knew I didn't have any money. I knew things were going to be tough, but that was my goal: to be a millionaire and to own my own business. The title of this chapter is "Poverty to Riches: Selling for Millions," and that's what I did.

Over my 36 years in business, I had three offers from people to purchase my business. The first came in 1969, when I'd been in business six years and had three stores. A fellow franchisee out of Louisiana offered me $450,000. That was a lot of money at the time; in today's dollars, that's probably about $4.5 million.

I told him, "No, I'll sell for $750,000."

He said no, he wouldn't pay me that much.

I said, "Fine. Have a good day."

The second offer came in 1988: I had a group of investors come and offer me $25 million. I had about 40 stores at the time. We worked at that and tried to negotiate, but it didn't work out.

In 1999, I received my third offer. At this point, I had 69 stores. I got an offer of $63 million, and I accepted it.

It was time to sell. In the Bible, in Ecclesiastes 3:1, it says, "To every thing there is a season, and a time to every purpose under the heaven." It was time to sell, and I knew it.

There was a time to grow and to build the business. That was 36 years before, when I was working on building and opening my first Burger King. Now, in 1999, it was the time to sell.

I had accomplished my goal many times over. I had made millions over the 36 years and enjoyed a great lifestyle. My family was blessed mightily by the Lord, and I had been making something happen in Burger King for 36 years. Now, I could sell my business for millions. I had accomplished my goal to be a millionaire.

Some people ask me, why did you sell? Why not keep operating and growing? You were making lots of money and doing what you loved.

There's one thing you have to understand in business: things go up and down. You have good years and bad years. My gut told me that it was time to sell.

I'd been up and down over the 36 years. I'd done extremely well—no complaints—but bad times come. In the bad times, you cannot sell if you want to sell and get out.

I felt it was time to get out. As it happens, fast food has struggled since 2000. I sold at the top.

I recently called a fellow franchisee, a very close personal friend of mine. He lives in Florida. He's a Burger King franchisee, and he's still operating his stores. He had about 25.

He said, "Murry, it's good to talk with you. You got out at the right time. The fun is gone. It's hard to make any money anymore; it's so competitive. I had to sell 12 of my stores just to survive." I think he operates 10 now.

He said, "I don't make any money. I pay the bills and get

enough money to buy some rice and beans to eat. The only positive thing is at least we're paying off the mortgages on these 10 sites. Within another 10 years, we'll have the mortgages paid off, so at least we'll own these 10 commercial sites. That's the positive side of it."

I said to myself, you know, nothing lasts forever.

The stock market doesn't go up forever, and it doesn't go down forever. Stormy weather doesn't continue day after day. It finally clears, doesn't it?

Sunny weather doesn't last day after day, either. Sooner or later, you're going to have some stormy weather.

The glory days of fast food are over. They're past. Yes, fast food is still a very strong, viable industry, but it is extremely competitive. The profit margins are much, much smaller than they used to be. Fast food is now at least 55 years old. That's an old industry. The rewards are much less now for the same investment of time and money in fast food.

I didn't say it was a bad industry; I'm just saying it's tough to make money in it. You've got to do a lot of hard work and invest a lot of money to make a little bit of money. You really don't want to be in that type of industry. I got into it at the right time, at the beginning of a new industry.

Norm Brinker, the founder of Chili's and Brinker International, told me that the way you want to make money is to get in on a new industry, or a new niche in an established industry. That's what he did when he opened Chili's.

After I sold, I never looked back. A lot of people look back and wonder, "Did I do right? Should I have kept this? Should I not have sold that?" I never second-guess myself.

Did I make the right decision to sell? I never thought

about that. I sold, and I walked away from it.

I did go into my former stores and have a Whopper, but I never judged how they were being operated. It wasn't my responsibility any longer. It belonged to the new owner. I had other responsibilities to handle.

I live my life each day, in the present and in the future. I don't waste time and energy looking back and second-guessing myself. I look forward. I have plenty on my schedule that I have yet to accomplish, so I don't waste time looking back.

Why did I write this book? My wife and kids have urged me for years to write a book about my Burger King story, ever since I sold my stores. I've just put it off and put it off. I said, "I'm not a writer."

But then, my good friend and colleague, Dr. Rahim, told me it was my destiny to write about my successful Burger King career. That hit me right between the eyes: my destiny.

He said that my story would be a blessing to many people, and that I should write it to instruct younger people on how to open a business, and the struggles and problems and adversities they would encounter, and how to be successful.

I finally did it, and actually, I've loved doing it. Now that I've written this book, I plan to write many more about life and business, the Lord willing. I pray that this book has been a real blessing to you.

About the Author

I'm a **real entrepreneur**—I love business. I have a knack for looking at a business and seeing ways for that business to improve, whether it's introducing new products, improving the services, or offering better value to the customer. I can immediately see where the bottlenecks are and what needs to change for the business to succeed.

As a franchisee and pioneer of fast food giant, Burger King, I built, developed, owned, and operated 69 restaurant locations from 1963 to 2000. Starting with only $40,000 of initial seed investment, I built a multi-state Burger King business, generating $815 million and serving 500 million customers.

As chairman and franchisor, I founded the Signs Now Corporation franchise system, which totaled 350 stores between 1986 and 2000. This business generated $150 million+ in revenues and was ranked #1 in the nation against all U.S.

franchisor companies by *Income Opportunities Magazine*.

Best of all, I loved what I did, so I never worked a day in my life.

Currently, I'm an international speaker and business consultant. I use my real-world experiences to offer help, advice, and inspiration to other entrepreneurs and their teams.

Finally, I want to say with humility, I am just an ordinary person, just like you. As you've read in this book, I was born poor. I didn't like being poor, so I got to work on changing that. I put together a plan and built my business, day by day, success upon success.

Along the way, I discovered that success is not a destination—it's a journey! I stand ready, and I am committed to helping you reach the next higher level of success on your journey.

If you go to my website, murryjevans.com, you can find out more about me.

Sign Up for My Newsletter

If you desire to receive information from me such as: new book releases, special book promotions, and periodic newsletters about life and business, then please leave me your valid email address here:
   http://murryjevans.com/newsletter-signup/

Thanks.

I promise you that I will not use your email to try to sell you other stuff! Doesn't that make you angry? It does me.

Your email will be used as stated above! Thanks for placing your confidence in my word.

Murry J. Evans

Help!

Please, I need you to do me a big favor. When you have time, go to Amazon and write a review on my book here:
   http://www.amazon.com/dp/1494743353/

Let me know what was helpful, inspirational, and a blessing to you. Your review will help me tremendously as I write the additional nine books, about life and business, that I have outlined.

Thanks so much for your help and time. Have a great day!

Quotes from four great captains of business that I have had the privilege and honor to work with

Always monitor your competitors, you'll never know what inspiration you may get. Give 'em a couple of bucks of your money and maybe learn how to make a million.
—Tom Ballinger

1. Loyalty is royalty. 2. Could you lend me $5 'til Friday?
—Ted Burke

Business is like driving bumper cars at the fair.
—Dewey Eason

You'll catch more fish if you leave your line in the water.
—Mark Evans

30% COMMISSION FEE

All third-party bookings will receive a 30% commission of my speaking and consulting fees. Please contact me here:
    info@murryjevans.com

Also, be sure and check out my website:
    murryjevans.com

Take care,
Murry

www.ingramcontent.com/pod-product-compliance
Lightning Source LLC
Chambersburg PA
CBHW051659170526
45167CB00002B/468